10 out of 12

Anne Washburn

A SAMUEL FRENCH ACTING EDITION

SAMUEL FRENCH

FOUNDED 1830

SAMUELFRENCH.COM
SAMUELFRENCH-LONDON.CO.UK

FOR PRODUCTION ENQUIRIES

UNITED STATES AND CANADA
Info@SamuelFrench.com
1-866-598-8449

UNITED KINGDOM AND EUROPE
Plays@SamuelFrench-London.co.uk
020-7255-4302

Each title is subject to availability from Samuel French, depending upon country of performance. Please be aware that *10 OUT OF 12* may not be licensed by Samuel French in your territory. Professional and amateur producers should contact the nearest Samuel French office or licensing partner to verify availability.

MUSIC USE NOTE

Licensees are solely responsible for obtaining formal written permission from copyright owners to use copyrighted music in the performance of this play and are strongly cautioned to do so. If no such permission is obtained by the licensee, then the licensee must use only original music that the licensee owns and controls. Licensees are solely responsible and liable for all music clearances and shall indemnify the copyright owners of the play(s) and their licensing agent, Samuel French, against any costs, expenses, losses and liabilities arising from the use of music by licensees. Please contact the appropriate music licensing authority in your territory for the rights to any incidental music.

IMPORTANT BILLING AND CREDIT REQUIREMENTS

If you have obtained performance rights to this title, please refer to your licensing agreement for important billing and credit requirements.

10 OUT OF 12 was first produced by the Soho Rep in New York City on May 26, 2015. The performance was directed by Les Waters, with sets by David Zinn, lights by Justin Townsend, sound by Bray Poor, costumes by Ásta Bennie Hostetter, and props by George Hoffman and Greg Kozatek. The Production Stage Manager was Amanda Spooner. The cast was as follows:

STAGE MANAGER	Quincy Tyler Bernstine
E3 (TECHIE)	Jeff Biehl
BEN/CHARLES	Gibson Frazier
COSTUME	Rebecca Hart
SIGET/OLD LADY/LUCILLE	Nina Hellman
EVA/MARIE	Sue Jean Kim
THE DIRECTOR	Bruce McKenzie
E2 (TECHIE)	Garrett Neergaard
SOUND	Bray Poor
JAKE/RICHARD	David Ross
PAUL/CARSTAIRS	Thomas Jay Ryan
ASSISTANT DIRECTOR	Conrad Schott
LIGHTS	Wendy Rich Stetson
JAMIE (ASM)	Leigh Wade

CHARACTERS

Some characters are both seen and heard on stage

BEN (plays **CHARLES**)

EVA (plays **MARIE**)

SIGET (plays **OLD LADY** and **LUCILLE**)

PAUL (plays **CARSTAIRS**)

JAKE (plays **RICHARD**)

ASM

Some characters are seen on the stage, but heard only in the house, or on headset:

THE STAGE MANAGER

AD

E2

These characters are only heard:

LIGHTS

SOUND

COSTUME

E3

E3 is in the booth, **E2** is in the house and then backstage,
ASM is mainly backstage.

SETTING

A technical rehearsal.

TIME

Three days.

IMPORTANT

Please note that when a character name is <u>underlined</u>, that exchange takes place over the headset.

AUTHOR'S NOTES

Beginning in the summer of 2005, I began jotting down notes during tech rehearsals. Those notes – direct or indirect quotations as well as observations – are incorporated throughout this play.

WHO IS ACTUALLY REAL AND WHO ISN'T:

In the Soho Rep production of this play, the audience was given headsets to listen in on the crew conversations which take place on headset (in the script, the character's name is underlined). Due to the limitations of those headsets, all of those conversations were pre-recorded. Speakers were placed throughout the house and conversations which took place in the house either took place live, or came through those speakers. Speaker conversations were either pre-recorded, or transmitted from a sound booth backstage.

LIGHTS, SOUND, COSTUME, and E3 were entirely pre-recorded.

STAGE MANAGER was generally a disembodied voice (sometimes transmitted live, sometimes pre-recorded) though we saw her crossing the stage once, and she was in the house to hand a lighter to the director.

All conversations which take place in the house with actors who we also see live on stage can either take place live, or through the speakers – this might depend on the stage/audience space of each production – but there presence should probably be a mix of the live and the disembodied.

A production could choose to include the designers as live actors stationed in the house but it should be made clear – through lights/sound/whatever – that their reality in the house space is not a continuous one.

OTHER

Whirrs indicate a lapse of some time. They probably sound like the whirr of a cassette tape being forwarded.

Page 77 – you can adjust the bum bum s to whatever piece of music you have selected

Licensees who wish to swap out specific New York theater references for local ones, please contact your licensing representative.

SPECIAL THANKS

The casts, creatives, and crews of: I Have Loved Strangers *performed at Williamstown by the Act 1 company,* Apparition *performed at The Connolly,* The Internationalist *at The Vineyard,* Orestes *at The Folger,* The Small *at the Ohio with Clubbed Thumb, and* Mr. Burns *at Playwrights Horizons. As well as the casts, crews and creatives of* **An Illiad** *at NYTW, Erin Courtney's* Map of Virtue *with 13P, the Fiasco Company's* Into The Woods *at Roundabout, and The Civilians'* Pretty Filthy, *all of whom allowed me to drop in on a bit of their techs.*

Jane Cox, Amy Ehrenberg, Kyle Gates, Rachael Hauck, Lisa Peterson, Bray Poor, Leigh Silverman Amanda Spooner, Justin Townsend, Charles Turner have all been especially generous with their time and thoughts.

Thanks to the Clubbed Thumb Writer group and extra extra thanks to Emma Griffin, for turning me on to the secret world of the headsets.

I would especially like to thank the following Bats for allowing me to workshop the play with them: Dominique Brillon, Jimmy Dailey, Alex Gould, Marlowe Holden, Lindsley Howard, Artem Kreimer, Rory Kulz, Leemore Malka, Zac Moon, Emily Olcott, Alex Seife, Kate Thulin, Paul Thomas Truitt, Colin Waitt, as well as Director Rachel Karp.

And the Guggenheim Foundation.

1.
PRE-SHOW

(There are neat furrows of carpentry rubbish – sawdust, screws, rubbishy wood bits, candy wrappers, etc. – and the **ASM** *is alternately sweeping them into a dustpan, and vacuuming the stage.)*

(Dustpan is being dumped into a big black garbage bag on stage.)

ASM. *(To her headset.)* Yeah, I'll be right there.

*(**ASM** goes offstage.)*

(After a long while she returns, and continues to sweep and vacuum.)

(There is a low muttering hum coming from all the speakers in the space, an utterly unintelligible murmuring.)

*(**E2** crosses, holding a bundle of electrical cording.)*

(Gradually we do hear a faint but distinct intermittent stream of instruction from **LIGHTS** *and* **SOUND**. *We will continue to hear this, steadily, evenly, until the play begins.)*

1.5
TEST TEST TESTING TEST TEST TEST

(We hear **JAMIE** *and the* **ASM** *over the headset.)*

STAGE MANAGER. Jamie are you on headset? Check, check, Jamie you there?

ASM. I'm here!

STAGE MANAGER. Great, thanks. Are you on headset Erik? Erik you there?

ASM. Erik's not on yet, he's still changing into his blacks.

STAGE MANAGER. Great, I'll come back to him. Joel? Do we have Joel?

E3. Here!

STAGE MANAGER. Okay excellent.

(Sound of a channel switch.)

STAGE MANAGER. *(Different tone and tenor entirely.)* Do I have Lights?

LIGHTS. You do.

STAGE MANAGER. Wonderful. And who is programming for you today?

LIGHTS. Tim but he's in the bathroom, here you want to test his headset yah?

STAGE MANAGER. I do.

LIGHTS. Let me just…

(Sound of fumbling, slightly different background hum.)

LIGHTS. Alright this is Tim, you good?

STAGE MANAGER. Wonderful. Thanks Julie!

LIGHTS. Thanks Molly.

STAGE MANAGER. Alright, Sound? Sound?

(This next line is heard, not in the headset, but in the house.)

STAGE MANAGER. Robert can you pick up your headset please? I just want to run a brief test.

SOUND. Oh right, sure.

   (Headset fumbling.)

<u>SOUND</u>. How's this you got me?

<u>STAGE MANAGER</u>. We have you. Thank you so much.

<u>SOUND</u>. Sure thing.

2.
OUR PLAY BEGINS

(At once, the muttering hum rises in volume: all conversations are audible for a second or two then:)

LIGHTS. Going dark!

(Darkness. Babble ceases.)

(After a moment, Vacuuming stops.)

ASM. *(Slight sarcasm.)* Thank you dark!

LIGHTS. *(Quietly.)* Lights Go.

(Lights do something incredibly vivid, and comprehensive.)

SOUND. Sound in the house!

(As does sound.)

3.
HALF HOUR

(Sound cuts out. Lights change.)

(House lights up again on low.)

*(**E2** is far upstage on the floor of the pink room with a screwgun working on a wall or repairing a hinge or something. There is a bag of chips by his side.)*

(The vacuum stands alone on the stage.)

(As:)

STAGE MANAGER. Ladies and Gentlemen welcome to our tech rehearsal. We are at half hour. Actors please make sure you're signed in. We'll be starting from the top of show in thirty minutes. Once again Ladies and Gentlemen, we are at half hour. Please make sure you're signed in.

AD. Thank you half hour.

E3. Erik?

E2. Uh huh.

E3. What is that you're eating?

E2. Pink salty gross things.

E3. That's what it looks like from up here. Well I won't say what it looks like. Okay: it looks fetal.

E2. I think they're shrimp…shrimp chips. Or crab? They were just lying here. *(Rustle of package.)* Yes, shrimp. That's why they're pink. They're Japanese.

E3. *Oh.* Oh. Japanese. Right. Are they good?

E2. Um…they're crunchy.

(In the house:)

LIGHTS. I'm starving.

SM. Do you want an apple? I have apples.

LIGHTS. No. I want… *(Abstractedly.)* something bad.

…

When was the last time you had a Funyun?

SM. Oh. My God. Years. Years. *(Beat.)* You want a Funyun?

LIGHTS. I haven't had a Funyun for five years. That weird forever long horrible aftertaste. *(Small pause.)* I don't want a Funyun. *(Calls out:)* Erik what's that you're eating?

>   *(**E2** looks up.)*

(Calls:) Nevermind, I don't want it. I don't.

SM. Jamie, everyone signed in?

ASM. All hands on deck.

SM. Wonderful. And how is everyone doing?

ASM. Siget is still in street clothes, she has a question about her skirt.

SM. Is Beth down there?

ASM. She was here just a moment ago, I'm currently tracking her down. Also it's muggy down here. I talked with Chip earlier and he's bringing in fans and we're going to plug them in as soon as we're done with the curling iron.

SM. Alright.

>   *(A moody cello – which then cuts out abruptly.)*

>   *(The moody cello again, at a lower level. Continues to play for a while.)*

LIGHTS. Can I see 116@70?

Add group 17

Add group 16@50

Update.

>   *(As:)*

>   *(Cello replaced with crickets. Crickets cut out.)*

>   *(After a pause: a new set of harder driving crickets.)*

Folks, we're going dark.

>   *(Darkness.)*

>   *(Lighting business around the footlights.)*

(Again, this is over the headset:)

<u>E2</u>. You know what I realize? Every tech, at the end of every tech, I end up with bruises, right on my thigh, from bumping into the seats in the dark.

<u>E3</u>. You should get your vitamin C levels checked.

<u>E2</u>. Really? Is that it?

<u>E3</u>. Yeah. Or D or B.

<u>E2</u>. Huh.

<u>ASM</u>. Are you bruised already?

<u>E3</u>. Yeah that's sort of extreme. That's more like leukemia.

<u>E2</u>. Yeah not yet but I just recalled. What is to come.

> (**LIGHTS** *up again as before.*)

> (**E2** *resumes drilling. Completes drilling. Walks into the wings.*)

> (**SOUND** *of a wood at night: crickets, cicadas, frogs.*)

> (*Silence.*)

> (**SOUND** *of the wood but with wilder elements added.*)

DIRECTOR. Hey Robert?

SOUND. Yo.

DIRECTOR. Which scene is this? You're messing with.

SOUND. Imps with index cards.

DIRECTOR. It should be more tropically at this point, ya?

SOUND. I thought this was pretty tropically. In the arc.

DIRECTOR. Could it be a little more tropically? What about that jaguar?

SOUND. I added that later on, then I deleted it.

DIRECTOR. Could we add it back in?

SOUND. In this scene?

DIRECTOR. Yah?

SOUND. Isn't it cheesy?

DIRECTOR. Is it?

SOUND. Isn't it?

DIRECTOR. Further away. More in the distance.

SOUND. I will give it a whirl.

DIRECTOR. Kind of obscuréd. Thank you.

SOUND. Do you want to specify where?

DIRECTOR. At your discretion.

    For the moment.

    We'll probably remove it. Ultimately.

SOUND. Gotcha.

E2. Joel did you pick up that exacto from the table or did someone else?

E3. Nope.

E2. It's not there at all.

> *(There's a low drone for a moment, then it fades out.)*
>
> *(Something shifts with the* **LIGHTS**, *shifts back.)*
>
> *(New insect* **SOUND**.*)*

E2. Did anyone pick up a yellow box cutter exacto knife from this table?

AD. Robert are those cicadas?

SOUND. Uh huh.

AD. Thought so.

    I remember the first time I saw a cicada. I was four. I thought it was an alien.

SOUND. They're big.

> *(Cicada sound speeds up.)*

    Take it to 40.

> *(Cicada sound pumps up.)*

E2. *(Low and half under breath, singing:)* Did you pick up that exacto from the table
Because without it I am not able

To…do my tasks, all of my tasks
As I am asked

(**ASM** *is vacuuming again.*)

(*Noise effect up fulsomely.*)

SOUND. Could you give more bottom to that thunder cue? Can you fill out the bottom?

(*Pause.*)

(*Singing abstractedly.*)

"BIG BOTTOM, MY GAL'S GOT 'EM"

(*Interrupts self.*) Oh and totally kill the u.b. 12.

STAGE MANAGER. And Elliott this mag light is for you.

DIRECTOR. Oh is that my mag light? Oh good.

STAGE MANAGER. You see, it clicks on and off up here.

DIRECTOR. On and off.

STAGE MANAGER. Yup.

DIRECTOR. Won-derful.

(*Sound again, with more bottom.*)

(*There is a weird tiny twirl of very beautiful female singing, something old and complicated sounding.*)

ASM. Hey could we have another table back here?

STAGE MANAGER. Why do you need another table?

ASM. Wardrobe wants it.

STAGE MANAGER. There should be – hang on.

SOUND. (*A general and casual announcement.*) Very Loud Sound in the house.

(*Completely overpowering noise.*)

(*Lights dim and oddly specific angular light thing happens only in the very corner of the stage.*)

(*Fades out.*)

STAGE MANAGER. Jamie, I'm on my way.

(…)

(Repeats, with a small difference.)

(Fades out.)

(Lights up in general.)

(The **STAGE MANAGER** *climbs up onto the stage. Crosses off.)*

(As we hear the sound of a drill from behind the set.)

4.
FIVE MINUTES

(A mild whirr as we jump forward in time.)

(A footlight kindles on.)

STAGE MANAGER. Ladies and Gentlemen we're at five minutes. Five minutes for places at top of show. five minutes.

> *(As:)*

> *(***EVA*** *bobs briefly into view from the wing, half in costume [big skirt], looks into house, bobs back in.)*

> *(***E2*** *enters again from side, stares up at grid again, and crosses off.)*

> *(As:)*

> *(The sound of electrical tape being unscrolled in the house.)*

> *(As:)*

LIGHTS. Alright Mr. Foster please show me…group 601 please

277 at full

group 60 out

hmmm.

Okay yeah so show me group 60 focused on the chandelier, at full…uh huh…

in white

at 50

at 30

at 70

> *(The footlight dims.)*

> *(As:)*

DIRECTOR. Are we still waiting for the Sound to build?

STAGE MANAGER. Yes we are.

STAGE MANAGER. Jamie you good for me to call Places? Is everything good for Places?

ASM. We need just a few more minutes. Siget is still getting her skirt worked out and we just tripped breaker #9 so I'm going to go fix it.

SM. Is this the fans?

ASM. Ben brought in one of those electric teapots and he forgot and plugged it in. We talked about it.

SM. When you have a moment, make a little sign.

ASM. *(Affirmative.)* I'm gonna make a little sign.

RECORDED FEMALE VOICE. *(Very Loud and sudden and out of nowhere.)* "Hello!"

(Softer.) "Hello and welcome to –" *(Offstage.)*

> *(Something with the light.)*

> *(Something with the light.)*

"Hello, and welcome to Soho Repertory Theatre. Please take this moment to turn off your electronic devices completely – the vibrate setting is audible in a theater this size, and fellow audience members *and* actors find the light of your LED screens distracting in the event of an emergency" *(Cuts out.)*

…

"In the event of an emergency please return the way you entered."

"Thank you and enjoy the show"

A VOICE WHICH WE DON'T KNOW WHERE IT COMES FROM IT IS DISTINCT. Please retrace your steps. Through fire. While screaming

> *(JAKE enters the house in near [but not completely] total period costume. He scans underneath the seats in a section of the first few rows.)*

JAKE. *(In a low voice.)* Molly no one found a phone around here did they?

STAGE MANAGER. No, but we'll keep an eye out.

JAKE. Thanks Molly.

SOUND. I've seen people not only text during shows, but hold the phone up to see it better.

LIGHTS. I grabbed a phone out of a teenager's hands. She was texting during the entire show. I grabbed it and I placed it under my butt.

> *(Meanwhile:)*
>
> **(JAKE** *appears onstage, shades his eyes and looks out at house, returns offstage.)*
>
> *(A conversation in the far back of the auditorium which is unintelligible.)*
>
> *(Rustle of package.)*
>
> **(BEN** *has appeared on stage.)*

DIRECTOR. Ben is this your shirt?

BEN. I have two shirts. This one, and a bluer stripier one. This one is the one I thought we decided we like the most.

DIRECTOR. Do we like that shirt the most?

COSTUME. We do.

DIRECTOR. Alright. Love it.

COSTUME. Do you want me to bring the other one back again? We can see it again.

DIRECTOR. *(Beat.)* No. *(Beat.)* I love it.

BEN. I like this one.

DIRECTOR. You do, do you.

BEN. I do.

DIRECTOR. Then I change – no. We can still go with that shirt. Although now I question my taste and judgment.

> **(BEN** *salutes smartly, and removes himself from the stage.)*

What are we waiting for now?

STAGE MANAGER. So we're still waiting for them to get into Costume.

STAGE MANAGER, Jamie how much longer.

ASM. We're like two minutes away

STAGE MANAGER. Ten minutes.

DIRECTOR. I'm no longer ready.

> *(A time passes. There are sounds. Some lassitude.)*

E3. *(Half absentmindedly, half deliberately introducing a tune:)* Du du *du* du du du, du du *du* du du

E2. He is rockin'

E3 AND E2. an anti solar, *attitude/*

STAGE MANAGER. Guys.

E3 AND E2. *(Really digging into it.)* Let the /Light

STAGE MANAGER. *(We should hear this in the house as well.)* GUYS

Wrong channel guys.

E3. O!

E2. Sorry!

STAGE MANAGER. Keep it cool, fellahs.

E3. Right right!

> *(Some sort of mechanical click as they presumably switch to another channel.)*

LIGHTS. Going dark on stage.

> *(Dark. In the dark:)*

AD. Is it drafty in here? My knee caps are cold.

My kneecaps get cold when it's drafty.

> *(Very loud: the cry of a jaguar.)*

5.
FIRST CUE

(Mild whirr as we make a slight hiccup forward in time.)

(Dramatic light switch and we see on stage:)

*(**EVA** in a big skirt and a hoodie for warmth upstage talking, low, to **DIRECTOR** who stands near her. We can't hear her.)*

(His arms are crossed, he's nodding a bit.)

*(Unconsciously she rearranges her skirt around her, she continues talking; he's listening, though he sometimes looks at the floor. The **AD** hovers nearby, listening and looking uncertain.)*

*(Downstage is **BEN**, bored, staring into his cell phone.)*

*(**SIGET**, an actress in an even bigger skirt, is pacing precisely along the upstage wall, trailing her hand along it absently. When she comes to the door she stops in front of it. Opens it part way in a speculative fashion, peers into the dark backstage, closes it.)*

(Stands in front of it.)

(Opens it again, this time a little wider, closes it again, continues pacing slowly and deliberately along the back wall, heaving her skirt about a bit as she does so.)

(As:)

STAGE MANAGER. Jamie you all set backstage?

ASM. Ready.

STAGE MANAGER. Erik?

E2. On my way.

STAGE MANAGER. Fantastic.

STAGE MANAGER. Folks, we'll be beginning in just a moment.

> *(As:)*
>
> *(A bright wadge of light materializes on the floor two feet away from him.)*
>
> *(**BEN** takes one long step sideways and enters it, shades his eyes, to the house:)*

BEN. This for me?

LIGHTS. *(Abstracted.)* No but stay…stay there for a moment if you would.

> *(**BEN** stays. He bobbles briefly. Sticks a foot out at an absurd angle. Retracts it. Stands.)*
>
> *(The light intensity changes.)*
>
> *(The wadge narrows, so that it disincludes him.)*

LIGHTS. Mkay.

> *(**BEN** takes one long step sideways back to his old position.)*
>
> *(**EVA** and the **DIRECTOR** have finished their conversation and he's returned to the auditorium.)*
>
> *(**EVA** stretches vaguely.)*

SOUND. We're good to go I think.

STAGE MANAGER. Fabulous. Julie?

LIGHTS. Lights is waiting.

STAGE MANAGER. Elliott? We're ready?

DIRECTOR. Yup.

STAGE MANAGER. Ladies and Gentlemen, I want to thank you for your work so far and thank you in advance for your patience during what will be a long process

Actors, you already know this, but this is your time to say "I can't see," "I need help," "I'm terrified."

Places for top of show. Places for top of show please.

(Actors slide off the stage.)

(Stage is bare.)

STAGE MANAGER. Standing by backstage. Standby Lights 101 – 102, house Lights, and Sound 1-3.

STAGE MANAGER. Quiet in the house.

STAGE MANAGER. House to half and Sound 1 – go

(House lights at half. Moody cello begins to play.)

House out and Sound 2 – go

(House lights out, and sound of a light breeze, birdsong.)

Lights 101. Go

(There's a long pause, bare stage.)

(The lights are dimming very very slowly.)

DIRECTOR. This is the count?

STAGE MANAGER. This is the count.

(At this point the stage is almost black.)

*(The **ACTORS** enter in the dim, situate themselves.)*

Lights 102. Sound 3 – Go

(There's a big pop sound, like an old fashioned flash bulb going off.)

(And the lights are up very sudden, bright and hot on:)

*(**EVA**, right at the edge of the stage, in a late Victorian taffeta dress with a big skirt – holding a tea cup in one hand and saucer in another.)*

*(**BEN**, similarly attired, standing back behind her a few paces; he is reading a letter.)*

(A slightly surreal twittering of birds, a play of leafy light: a lush garden.)

*(**EVA** is watching Charles.)*

EVA. *(Rather loud.)* Charles.

> *(His head jolts up, a look of almost panic on his face.)*

Were you listening, Charles?

DIRECTOR. Okay, no.

STAGE MANAGER. Ladies and Gentlemen we're going to hold.

> *(The actors slump slightly.)*

LIGHTS. What do you think?

DIRECTOR. Well… I think it's disgusting, unfortunately.

LIGHTS. Too much visibility?

DIRECTOR. It looks like the beginning of a play.

LIGHTS. Right…

DIRECTOR. Why did I think a dim was preferable to a good old-fashioned blackout.

LIGHTS. Why indeed.

DIRECTOR. I know why: because there is no such thing as a good old fashioned black out.

Is there *no way* to eliminate that exit light?

STAGE MANAGER. *(Confirming.)* We can't eliminate the exit light.

> *(A pause.)*

DIRECTOR. One day. I'm going to eliminate that exit light.

STAGE MANAGER. *(Pleasantly.)* Not on my watch.

DIRECTOR. That's one square foot of masking standing between me, and theatrical bliss Richter.

STAGE MANAGER. We're not covering the exit light.

LIGHTS. Remember that the aisle lights aren't on. They're broken. So that's going to be part of the overall light bleed profile as well.

DIRECTOR. When are they being fixed?

STAGE MANAGER. The guy is coming in on Monday so we can get them up before first preview.

DIRECTOR. And they can't just *stay* broken until…July?

STAGE MANAGER. They can't.

DIRECTOR. Where is the love. Dr. Ford – do what you can.

What I feel about that *cello* is that I could not hate it more.

It was my idea, and I could not have come up with a more underwhelming one.

SOUND. It is a bit solemn.

DIRECTOR. In a way I want them to enter with nothing but then I think no, we aren't *German.*

I mean I'm right, right? It needs a little something-something.

SOUND. A little something-something.

DIRECTOR. Something.

SOUND. Let me play around with something.

DIRECTOR. Play around with it.

> *(A brief snatch of song, more or less just for himself.)*

> *Ist eine hunst die far die Flabbergast*

> *(As:)*

> *(**SOUND** sets up new sequence.)*

What about that count. At the top.

LIGHTS. …It's long.

Shall we try a six count?

DIRECTOR. It's very long. It might be good. Let's keep it for the moment I want to see it again.

LIGHTS. Got it.

DIRECTOR. But it's long.

LIGHTS. Uh huh.

STAGE MANAGER. We ready?

LIGHTS. Lights is ready.

SOUND. Need a sec more.

DIRECTOR. *(A brief snatch of song, in a deep harsh German accent, more or less just for himself.)*
  IST EINE HUNST DIE FAR DIE FLABBERGAST
  IST SWEINHUNST DIE FI HEIN HEINST.
  IST EINE HUNST DIE FAR DIE FLABBERGAST
  IST SWEINHUNST DIE FI HEIN HEINST.
  FINISH IS "IST MEIN
  IST MEIN"

SOUND. Okay good to go.

STAGE MANAGER. Excellent.

  Elliot, we're ready to go.

DIRECTOR. Eva, my darling; Ben, my dearest, I think we need to try getting you there in the pitch dark. Let me know what we can do to help you with that.

EVA. In the pitch dark?

DIRECTOR. More or less.

EVA. Okay. Cool.

  *(While all that is happening; the **ACTORS** onstage:)*

  *(**BEN** looks up into the lights. Looks over stage right.)*

  *(**EVA** swivels towards him, in a dramatic fashion, swirling her skirt as she does so.)*

  (She turns back, pulls her skirt back farther the other way, and then reswivels, shoving the skirt forward as she does so, so as to get a maximum effect.)

  (She may do this a few more times, not so much pantomiming a passionate swirl, as scientifically exploring and attempting to exacerbate the effects of it.)

  *(**BEN**, watching, lifts his hands above his head, cups them, and pantomimes a few flamenco claps. Maybe does a few shuffly foot movements.)*

(EVA chats with BEN in a low voice, as she does so unconsciously chunking the cup and saucer against each other, rim to rim, in a slow, methodical, but definite fashion.)

(SIGET emerges briefly, peers out into the house, returns backstage.)

(Through all of this there are a few odd lunges of sound.)

STAGE MANAGER. Okay guys we're going to stand by to go back to the top of the show and go through your entrances again, this time in the dark. Jamie and Erik are going to be standing backstage to assist you.

(The lights have shifted from the bright pop light to a neutral wash on stage, and the house lights.)

Places please, Ladies and Gentlemen, places.

(EVA and BEN drift offstage.)

STAGE MANAGER. Everyone in position back there?

ASM. All good.

STAGE MANAGER. Standing by backstage. Standby Lights 101 – 102, house Lights, and Sound 1-3.

STAGE MANAGER. Quiet in the house.

STAGE MANAGER. House to half and Sound 1 – go

(There's a long pause, bare stage.)

(Slowly, lightly, in the distance, a bit of maybe banjo noodling. [By 'banjo' I don't mean a country twang kind of sound, I mean the banjo in its other incarnation as an eerier lighter nimbler instrument than the guitar, darker.])

House out and Sound 2 – go

(House lights out, and sound of a light breeze, birdsong.)

Lights 101. Go

(The noodling slowly resolves itself into a melody, kind of driving and eerie, and the volume increases. The sound is definitely coming from backstage, from a specific location, and then abruptly is on the overhead speaker.)

(At this point the stage is black.)

STAGE MANAGER. Sound 2.5. Go

(A cityscape rises in volume. New York at rush hour, Times square, cars, horns, shouting, hawking.)

Lights 102. Sound 3 – Go

(There's a big pop sound, like an old fashioned flash bulb going off.)

(And the lights are up very sudden, bright and hot on:)

(EVA, *somewhere in the middle of the stage and* **BEN** *where he was before.)*

(A slightly surreal twittering of birds, a play of leafy light: a lush garden.)

E3. Reality: 1. Fantasy: 0.

(BEN *looks around, site-ing himself, shifts a step or two to his left, and then back.)*

DIRECTOR. Well…that's no good.

STAGE MANAGER. Hold.

(EVA *has raised her hand.)*

DIRECTOR. Yah?

EVA. I can't see a damn thing.

DIRECTOR. Yah, I can see that.

BEN. You know there was that bright bright light then there wasn't a lot of time to adjust.

EVA. I didn't have the first clue.

BEN. Maybe if we had time to adjust.

DIRECTOR. And all I could see was the radiant glare from my enemy the exit sign. And then actors, stumbling around on stage in a radiant glare.

EVA. Do you know what it was like? It was like that Edgar Allen Poe story. Where the man is in the dark, and he knows there's a pit.

DIRECTOR. Eva we're going to resituate you, further from the yawning gap. I'm a big fan of actors not plummeting into the audience.

EVA. Me too.

DIRECTOR. I mean they've paid real money. And look at Eva there, at least two hundred pounds, and all those pointy bits.

Can we also get tiny dots of glowtape on the edge of the stage? Tiny ones.

E2. *(Low, muttered.)* He doesn't *know* there's a pit. He *finds out* there's a pit.

DIRECTOR. Ben I think you can stay as you are.

Beth?

COSTUME. Yes.

DIRECTOR. Night vision goggles, for the actors. It's a good look, yah? It's steampunk, am I right?

COSTUME. I'm not feeling it.

DIRECTOR. Eat your carrots people, eat your carrots.

STAGE MANAGER. Guys you can handle this dark.

> *(The **ASM** has emerged from backstage with a roll of glow tape on her wrist like a bracelet. She is carrying a small hole puncher. She kneels down and punches out dots of glow tape that she carefully affixes to the very lip of the stage.)*

BEN. And hey Jamie, maybe I could get some tape here? For my mark?

DIRECTOR. Ben I think we don't want a nasty glowing blot. Right in the middle of my hard won dark. Not if it's not a question of life or death.

STAGE MANAGER. You're on your mark Ben.

BEN. I am. But it's strictly by chance.

DIRECTOR. I've got a lot of faith in you Ben.

STAGE MANAGER. And Eva we're going to resituate you.

> *(The door in the wall upstage opens and **SIGET** peeps out. The door closes again. After a while she emerges from offstage; she has a vast skirt. She is also carrying a tea cup, and saucer.)*
>
> *(She joins **BEN** and **EVA** who are chatting.)*
>
> *(The three of them stand chatting.)*
>
> *(Somehow – probably it flows from gesturing, which exaggerates – **BEN** and **SIGET** and **EVA** are squaring off with their tea items, a kind of slow motion cup and saucer combat in which they are careful not to actually impact the items with any force, but also careful to make enough contact so that there is a tiny distinct 'clink.')*
>
> *(Meanwhile:)*

E2. I have to say that there's a real small part of me that thinks a motorcycle wouldn't be the worst purchase I'd ever made.

ASM. It'd be close.

E2. It'd be close.

STAGE MANAGER. Eva can we have you at position please.

> *(**EVA** leaves off the teacup clinking, walks to mid-stage.)*

EVA. Where –

hereish?

DIRECTOR. Thereish to the left a pace and back a pace.

> *(She does this.)*

Another half pace.

> *(She does that.)*

That's fine, right?

LIGHTS. Yup.

STAGE MANAGER. Eva please hold while we relight you.

> *(Lights up bright on* **EVA.***)*
>
> *(Then brighter.)*
>
> *(Then some other change.)*
>
> *(We're also hearing toggling.)*

EVA. This light is so bright.

> …

I feel that it's judging me.

DIRECTOR. The light is just doing its job. *I'm* judging you. Judging you, and finding you wanting.

> *(***EVA*** sticks tongue out.)*

Oh that's nice. There will be one more light, right in your eyes.

EVA. Excellent.

DIRECTOR. And small spikes, right in the stage.

EVA. Excellent.

LIGHTS. Alright Richter we're good.

STAGE MANAGER. Alright. Eva, would you step forward?

> *(She does so.)*

Forward. Okay can you feel it?

EVA. Uh huh.

STAGE MANAGER. So it's back a tick.

EVA. Uh huh.

STAGE MANAGER. Now you know. Now you know, when you've gone too far.

DIRECTOR. *(Absently.)* Would that we *all* had a glarey light. To let us know when we've gone too far.

> *(While* **LIGHTS** *is working:)*
>
> *(***JAKE*** is in the first row chatting with the* **AD***:)*

AD. Hey.

JAKE. Hey.

AD. So Elliott asked me to pass these on to you.

JAKE. These are notes?

AD. Line notes.

JAKE. Cool. Cool.

AD. This one, I noticed you tend to get this one wrong, I think it might be a habit at this point so…

JAKE. Uh huh.

AD. And it was actually one that Carla asked me to specifically mention to you.

JAKE. Cool.

AD. She said it's a moment where the precise language is really important so. You know, playwrights. And you've kind of been. You tend to *approximate* it.

JAKE. Uh huh. Okay well, great man. I'll look at it.

AD. And if you ever have any, you know, questions or anything I mean. Feel free. In case Elliott isn't available or whatever. I mean obviously I'm not going to have an answer for everything but I can give it a shot.

JAKE. Um…okay then.

AD. Great, man. Yeah, just let me know.

JAKE. Will do.

SOUND. I just bought this sweater and I think I hate it. I can't tell you what it is to wear a sweater I hate as much as I hate this one.

COSTUME. No I know what you mean. God.

SOUND. I mean I'm right, right? It's *that* bad.

COSTUME. Um…

SOUND. You can tell me.

COSTUME. I guess it depends on who you are. And I don't know you well enough, so…

SOUND. Yeah. I hate it.

> (At **DIRECTOR**: *Would that we all had a glarey light, to let us know when we've gone too far.*)

STAGE MANAGER. Alright we're due for a ten. Take ten everyone

BEN. Thank you ten

(A general muttering:)

Thank you ten

EVA. Thanks ten!

(As everyone trails off:)

THAT SAME VOICE WHICH WE DON'T KNOW WHERE IT COMES FROM IT IS DISTINCT. Thank you for this gift of time – which is not yours to give. Thank you for stars, for space, for the pounding of my heart, for tender spring and this first evanescing summer for the wild fall for holy words the glitter of my breath in the winter for a surging of hope for a moment of peace for glances which make everything pause thank you for my every shuddering orgasm. This is sarcasm. *Thank you.* Ten.

6.
DO IMPS EAT APPLESAUCE?

(We whirr forward a bit in time.)

*(An **OLD LADY**, in a big rocker.)*

(She is dressed all in black, and a black veil covers her face.)

*(**BEN** stands nearby, at a respectful distance.)*

(The garden soundtrack from before has become thicker, morphy, foresty.)

OLD LADY. Did he have a prayer book, among his effects?

CHARLES. Not among them, no. But I have no reason to believe that every single one of his possessions were retained.

OLD LADY. *(Intake of breath.)* You do not think that they would...from one of their comrades...that they would *steal*.

CHARLES. I do not think that they would regard it as stealing, precisely. Sailors have a notoriously fluid notion of property. And they drink a great deal, many of them and that makes them, worse men sometimes than they really know how to be.

OLD LADY. Do you think that Richard drank a great deal?

(Over the next line:)

<u>**LIGHTS**</u>. Can we hold please.

STAGE MANAGER. Ladies and gents we're holding please.

DIRECTOR. Who's eating oranges?

COSTUME. Do you want a piece?

DIRECTOR. I want just a piece.

*(**SOUND** sneezes.)*

AD. *Gezunheit*

EVA. *Gezunheit*

COSTUME. Blez you.

SOUND. Thanks.

E3. I'm starving.

E2. I've got a sandwich.

E3. Is that what you're doing? Are you eating a sandwich?

E2. I'm not eating it right now.

E3. You sound muffled.

E2. Like you can't hear me?

E3. I can hear you. But it sounds a little like I'm hearing you through a sandwich.

(Sound of an adjustment.)

E2. How about now?

E3. Oh that's better.

E2. Let me know if you want half.

E3. Of your sandwich?

E2. If you're starving, you're welcome to half. It's in my backpack in the corner of the booth, the black one, top pocket. You're welcome to half.

E3. What kind of sandwich?

E2. Salami and swiss cheese.

E3. What kind of bread?

ASM. *(Laughing.)* I thought you were starving.

E3. I'm starving for something really good. Salami and swiss cheese *might* be really good but it teeters on the precipice of the question of the bread.

E2. Um… 7 grain.

E3. 7 grain, like, from where.

E2. From the store.

E3. The grocery store.

E2. The grocery store. Normal 7 grain bread.

E3. Toasted?

E2. No.

E3. Mustard?

E2. No. Just mayo. One leaf of lettuce.

(Judicious pause.)

E3. Okay I'm going to pass. But thank you Erik. You're a good man in a pinch.

DIRECTOR. *(Humming under his breath.)*

> *IST EINE HUNST DIE FAR DIE FLABBERGAST*
> *IST SWEINHUNST DIE FI HEIN HEINST.*
> *IST EINE HUNST DIE FAR DIE FLABBERGAST*
> *IST SWEINHUNST DIE FI HEIN HEINST.*
> *FINISH IS "IST MEIN*
> *IST MEIN"*

Are we?

STAGE MANAGER. Five minutes.

DIRECTOR. Oh never never mind.

Now I have a handful of orange peel.

LIGHTS. Getting better…hold here for a second please 266 out

delete 332

this is the state of 53 please

LIGHTS. and while we're at it we might as well look at that transition. That transition is rickety rickety rickety.

STAGE MANAGER. Julie you're going to work the transition as well.

LIGHTS. It's rickety.

STAGE MANAGER. Gotcha.

LIGHTS. Show me group 30 focused on the back wall please.

STAGE MANAGER. This is just your pro-forma reminder that at this rate we're not making it though the work list by the end of the day.

LIGHTS. This is not a surprise, surely.

STAGE MANAGER. Just your pro-forma reminder.

LIGHTS. I hear you.

STAGE MANAGER. Actors when we resume we're going to be taking it from the transition.

(In the house:)

JAKE. *(Plomping himself down.)* Hey.

EVA. Hey.

(Tiny bit of a pause.)

JAKE. So um…

EVA. "um…"?

JAKE. "Um." I'm wondering.

EVA. Uh huh?

JAKE. I'm wondering if um…if that could happen again. Maybe with dinner involved? First?

EVA. I like food.

JAKE. Food is just awesome.

DIRECTOR. With the playwright gone where's that little nimbus of panic and criticism right over by my left shoulder?

How am I to know that I'm getting everything very subtly wrong?

Are we still waiting on you, Julie?

LIGHTS. You are. 63 and 64 at 70.

STAGE MANAGER. We're going to need another minute.

DIRECTOR. I await your pleasure.

AD. Didn't Carla say she'd be back today?

DIRECTOR. She was overoptimistic.

I did not pray to the flu Gods. They move in their own very mysterious ways.

*(**AD** laughs heartily.)*

LIGHTS. Oh… I don't know. I just don't don't don't…know.

Oh I know!

Let's try group 81 at full – oh there it is look at that. Yes.

(Light change.)

(Meanwhile, on Stage:)

(**SIGET** *and* **BEN** *are running lines, with a few gestures.*)

(*While* **E2** *comes out from the wings and removes the rocking chair.*)

(*They still run lines in place, both standing.*)

(*In the house: someone is humming. Something from the '40s.*)

LIGHTS. um, group 26 – oh god – group 26 and group 381 at 161

at full

group 26 out

85 at full

undo 86 at full

Tim, are the focuses absolutely hot on 61 and 70? It feels a little bright in the center I'm wondering if there's way we can – just kill one? Kill 62?

don't kill 62.

kick it down by 10 points.

reverse 71? There we go. That's tidier.

then back that truck up.

and…we're good to go.

STAGE MANAGER. Super. Actors to the stage for the transition please.

DIRECTOR. You know I had a nightmare about this transition last night.

STAGE MANAGER. *This* one?

DIRECTOR. I *know*. I suppose it must remind me of a transition I had as a child.

(**BEN** *and* **SIGET** *drift off.*)

COSTUME. It's still so slow.

STAGE MANAGER. SO slow.

COSTUME. I can't even get Facebook. You know where it's terrible, Playwrights. Or was it Playwrights. Somewhere I've been recently. MCC?

STAGE MANAGER. I always feel like: there's no excuse, people. It's already a dark room full of electricity.

AD. *(Not clear who this is to.)* One of my teachers, if you fell asleep, he'd take his teeth out and place them on your desk. His falsies.

LIGHTS. The goal is still to do a run before first preview, right?

STAGE MANAGER. That's still the goal.

LIGHTS. I feel like that's entirely possible.

STAGE MANAGER. It's entirely possible. Eva to the stage please, Eva Anders to the stage.

> *(We hear her offstage initially as she darts on.)*

EVA. Here I am here I am here I am!

> *(She places herself.)*

I was tinkling.

STAGE MANAGER. That's what the break is for, Eva.

EVA. Oh sure. *(Charming:)* I was bored.

This is from?

STAGE MANAGER. From the knock.

EVA. The knock.

> *(She positions herself.)*

Knock away.

STAGE MANAGER. We ready?

LIGHTS. Ready-steady.

SOUND. I'm all in.

STAGE MANAGER. Erik?

E2. Ready to rumble.

STAGE MANAGER. Okay standby Lights 141 – 144

Standby Sound 32 – 37

Standby Erik

STAGE MANAGER. *(To* **EVA.***)* Okay we're all set.

STAGE MANAGER. Lights 141, Sound 32 – go.

> *(***EVA** *is sitting at a small writing desk, working furiously away at a letter. We hear the skritching of the pen on paper.)*

Erik – go.

> *(There is a gentle knock, on the wall.)*

Sound 32.7…

> *(***EVA** *pauses for a moment,)*

Go.

> *(The skritching sound stops.)*
>
> *(***EVA** *looks up,)*

Sound 33…

> *(And, after a moment.)*
>
> *(Resumes her writing.)*

Go.

> *(Skritching sound resumes.)*

Erik – go.

> *(A louder knock. A knocking.)*

Sound 33.5

Go.

> *(***EVA** *looks up; skritching sound stops.)*

Erik – go.

> *(A pounding on the wall.* **EVA***, startled, half tumbles from her chair and stands, rigid, in the middle of the room, staring at the wall.)*

Erik – cease.

> *(The pounding ceases, abruptly.)*
>
> *(A pause. A pause.)*

Wall, Lights 142 go, Sound 36 –

> *(The wall parts slightly, a misty light revealed.)*

Go.

> *(Lush forest sounds increasingly in volume and also a bit morphing into something jungle-ier.)*

> *(**EVA** is rigid with fear.)*

Lights 143 – go.

> *(blackout)*

Wall – go.

> *(There are dim sounds from the stage.)*

DIRECTOR. I can hear scuffling!

> *(There are dim sounds from the stage.)*

STAGE MANAGER. Lights 144 and Sound 37…

Go.

> *(Lights up on:)*

> *(An **OLD WOMAN** in a rocking chair with a black veil concealing her face.)*

> *(**BEN** is playing **CHARLES**.)*

DIRECTOR. That was a lot of scuffling!

STAGE MANAGER. Do you want to go back?

DIRECTOR. Do we need to go back?

STAGE MANAGER. Guys that was noisy, any problems?

E2. Just noisy!

ASM. Sorry!

STAGE MANAGER. We're fine.

DIRECTOR. *(In a thick Eastern European accent.)* Consider… yourselves…varned…

> *(**BEN** meanwhile has leaned over a bit to check that he's on his mark.)*

STAGE MANAGER. Moving on, ladies and gentlemen. Moving on.

(Light changes again, sound up, the garden soundtrack from before has become thicker, morphy, foresty.)

(There is a brief little pause.)

(The scene continues.)

OLD LADY. Did he have a prayer book, among his effects?

(Under this:)

STAGE MANAGER. Happy?

LIGHTS. Happyish. It's better. Happyish.
The blackout was late.

(A beat.)

STAGE MANAGER. Was it. Noted.

CHARLES. Not among them, no. But I have no reason to believe that every single one of his possessions were retained.

OLD LADY. *(Intake of breath.)* You do not think that they would…from one of their comrades…that they would *steal.*

CHARLES. I do not think that they would regard it as stealing, precisely. Sailors have a notoriously fluid notion of property. And they drink a great deal, many of them and that makes them, worse men sometimes than they really know how to be.

OLD LADY. Do you think that Richard drank a great deal?

CHARLES. I know for a fact, Ma'am, that he did not. Oh I'm sure he took a drop, from time to time. Most men do. And he would have been regarded, as unfriendly, if he did not.

OLD LADY. Unfriendly. No. That is one thing which could never be said about Richard, that he was an unfriendly boy. Or man.

Friendliness is generally counted as a great good, by other men, by mankind. A friendly man will not…

Fuck.

AD. Um… *(A great clattering.)* one second one second

OLD LADY. No I have it. I have it. He will not call you…

Fuck.

> (**AD** *has found the binder and leafing furiously through it.*)

STAGE MANAGER. To account for your faults.

AD. *(Almost at the same time with a tiny lag.)* To account for your faults.

OLD LADY. *To account for your faults.*

> *(Emphasis is about line remembering and not about intra scene dynamics.)*

He will enter into your vices and support your weaknesses out of fellowship.

I *(Ditto.) am not* and have never been a friendly woman. It would have been easier to be friendly, no, it would have been *simpler*, to be friendly. It would have been easier. *(as* **SIGET***:)* I do know this. *(as* **OLD LADY***:)* It has taken a great deal of effort, to be unfriendly. But I am much the better for it. It was a lesson Richard never could take. He rejected it with my milk I suppose. I couldn't nurse him, did you know that?

> *(Beat.)*

CHARLES. He never mentioned it.

OLD LADY. Well. I want to thank you for taking the trouble to come. To tell me of his burial.

CHARLES. There were a very few things in his possession and, I have given them to you – no no, I wouldn't want to part you from them. But I wonder if I might.

> *(Bit of a pause.)*

This will strike you as peculiar.

There is an old apple tree, in your orchard. Richard climbed upon it many times, as a boy.

OLD LADY. Oh, that *tree.* I couldn't keep him out of it. It was half rotten, and those apples never were worth eating.

CHARLES. He said that you forbad him to climb it – in all
good reason, as he recognized at the time. But that
tree, he said, was his delight, and he clambered up into
it whenever he could.

OLD LADY. He was my despair. Throughout his boyhood.
Daily. Daily he came to grief, in one way or another.
I think I punished him every single night.

CHARLES. He said that he nearly died, climbing that tree.
He was on an upper branch, almost at the top, and it
gave way suddenly

> *(The door in the upper wall opens,* **PAUL** *steps
> through, they turn towards him, he looks surprised
> to see them.)*

> *(***PAUL*** closes the door in a slow and absent
> manner.)*

Um… *(Running back through this bit pro-forma until he hits
a new section.)* He said that he nearly died, climbing that
tree. He had almost reached the top when the branch
gave way and he fell ten feet before he landed – only
by chance – onto a lower one. He landed directly onto
his stomach, the wind knocked right from him, and
then fell again but falling managed to catch hold of a
branch below and hung there, heaving for air, sure he
would let go, knowing he couldn't hang on, but hang
on he did, somehow, to this day he doesn't know how –
didn't know how – until finally, he caught his breath,
he gained the strength to haul himself up.

He lay on that branch in the crown of the tree until
nightfall watching the day wane. Thinking every hour
that this was an hour he might never have…existed.

It was spring, and he watched the dusk come through
a curtain of white blossoms. That the last light caught
them and they were translucent, gold, and then when
the sun faded they were ghosts, and fragrance – I'm
quoting him there, of course. He said he heard you
calling for him, and calling for him, and finally when

it was quite night he climbed down again, and came home. You were terribly angry, he said, and sent him to bed without his supper, but he never spent a happier evening listening to the voices of his family down by the fireside below.

I don't know if he ever told you that.

OLD LADY. Ah.

No. No he never did.

CHARLES. I would like. Very much. I would like to have a cutting, if I might, from that tree. A branch. I have an apple tree of my own, in my garden at home, and I could graft the cutting to it. There's a chance that it might take hold. I know this is an odd request.

OLD LADY. That *tree*. Lightning blasted it two years ago. It was half rotten and it burnt to the ground. They took out the stump this spring.

I'm very sorry, Mr. Westerly. I'm glad Richard had such a good friend.

CHARLES. Ah. Well. That is a disappointment, I confess it.

OLD LADY. Perhaps I can offer you one of his toys, from his time in the nursery, there was a lion on wheels, he would pull it with a string. I am fond of it, but there are other toys of his which bring up similar memories.

CHARLES. No. No ma'am you are too kind. I would not take from you any particular thing that had belonged to him. I'm sure that each one is precious in its way. I would have never raised the topic but for that apple tree.

OLD LADY. Well. It was kind of you to come.

(*The* **OLD LADY** *raises its veil, it's an imp.*)

(**CHARLES** *gasps.*)

LIGHTS. Can we hold here?

STAGE MANAGER. Hold please.

(*The actors slump.*)

DIRECTOR. That isn't the imp mask surely? That horrible thing?

COSTUME. It's an option for an imp mask.

DIRECTOR. *(Mildly.)* I hate it. Very very much.

COSTUME. It can go away. You did like it when it was a prototype.

DIRECTOR. I did. I did.

I did it was much it was rawer looking.

COSTUME. So rawer looking is good.

DIRECTOR. I think rawer looking is very good.

> *(To* LIGHTS.*)*

Doctor Ford.

LIGHTS. What are you thinking.

DIRECTOR. I think this is, *generally* right but I think

LIGHTS. Is this in the ballpark of what we were talking about?

DIRECTOR. I think it might be too ordinary

LIGHTS. Does it want to be *murkier*?

DIRECTOR. I think…no. I think that actually. I think that it wants to be just a little bit brilliant somehow, around the edges

LIGHTS. More…light…?

DIRECTOR. No, no, not a lot of light it seems like a scene which takes place in, the shadows or in a

LIGHTS. It's a parlor with all of the curtains drawn, right? Basically.

DIRECTOR. I don't think it's…the breakfast nook it isn't sunshine streaming in all around but I think…

I think the ending should be a surprise, to everyone.

LIGHTS. So a normal nothing spooky nothing impy

DIRECTOR. No, but there's that aurora of light, around an eclipse, you know what I'm taking about

> *(Micropause.)*

LIGHTS. Gotcha. Let me try something out.

DIRECTOR. Paul that isn't your shirt, is it?

> *(**PAUL** has, at some point before this, wandered out onto the set where he has been opening and closing the door very slowly, obliviously.)*

> *(**PAUL** stretches his arms wide, as if obediently, exposing his shirt to the house.)*

> *(It is silk, so old as to be a shade of yellow. And something has gone badly wrong with the sleeves.)*

DIRECTOR. Beth that isn't his shirt.

COSTUME. That's not the shirt.

> *(When **PAUL** speaks we recognize the distinct voice we heard earlier.)*

PAUL. This is my own shirt.

DIRECTOR. What happened to your shirt-shirt?

PAUL. I purchased this online. It belonged to a duke, of the period. And then I altered it a little. I thought it would be right if the cuffs were filthy.

> *(There's a bit of a beat.)*

E3. Guys…

ASM. Yup.

DIRECTOR. I feel that, something, which, very much characterizes Carstairs, is that he is a very fastidious dresser. Very, ah, correct.

PAUL. To all appearances. In the eyes of the world.

> *(Microbeat.)*

DIRECTOR. Yes.

PAUL. But do we see him. Do *we* [*gesture which is meant to generally encompass audience but also includes gestalt of entire creative team and the gods of the theater in general*] see him as the world sees him. Or do we see *deeper*.

> *(Microbeat.)*

DIRECTOR. Let's go with the actual shirt.

*(There's a moment where **PAUL** doesn't speak.)*

PAUL. *(Very slowly, very deliberately.)* Would you like me to change? Right now.

(Tiny beat.)

DIRECTOR. We'll move forward. But, in general, let's stick with the shirt as planned.

*(**PAUL** nods his head. Steps through the door and closes it behind him.)*

DIRECTOR. Can we take it from, from the tree moment.

*(**BEN** and **SIGET** are playing a game where he sticks his foot under the rocker and she gently tries to roll it on him and he tries to pull his foot away in time.)*

*(Maybe she gets him by mistake and there's concern and the **SM** butts in too, briefly.)*

STAGE MANAGER. Alright "he was my despair."

LIGHTS. I'm sorry, from "he nearly died."

STAGE MANAGER. My apologies. From "he nearly died."

*(**BEN** and **SIGET** reassemble themselves.)*

CHARLES. He said that he nearly died, climbing that tree. He was on an upper branch, almost at the top, and it gave way suddenly and he fell onto a lower one, ten feet below it, but only by chance.

*(We hear **PAUL** thinking.)*

PAUL. Put yourself to the test. Where are you? I am in my study. Carstairs' study. *My* study.

What do you hear?

*(We hear, from behind a flat, **BEN**: "It was spring, and he watched the dusk come through a curtain of white blossoms.")*

PAUL. That is not what I hear

*(**BEN**, continuing with the line, dwindles away swiftly.)*

PAUL. Those are not the sounds. Concentrate.

> *(There are new sounds: a clock, ticking in a study,*
> *a faint but distinct clopping of horses in a street*
> *outside.)*

Alright. I am in my study. I open my eyes. What do I see?

A wallpaper. An exquisite wallpaper. Extremely expensive.

I chose it myself this particular paper I make those selections I do not consider the act feminine, on the contrary. *A man creates the world around him.* And to do so he must see ruthlessly.

I must see. Ruthlessly.

Even the most particular eye dulls with the days, with the passage of – dulls with the days. And it has been years, I now realize, since I have looked, really looked, at the paper.

Hands pressed to the paper. Carstairs' hands, pressed to the paper. My hands, pressed to the paper. Describe the hands, your hands, these are your hands:

They are large hands. There is something broad, about them, almost the hands of a laborer, hammish. But not. Ham. Hands. There is force in them, tension in them, delicacy, in them.

They are hands which understand, tactics. Hands capable of almost indescribable subtleties. Upon the keys of a pianoforte. Upon the bodies of women.

Describe the paper. Upon which these hands are pressed. See it. Really, truly, *see* it.

It is dimmed, with cigar smoke. And time and lesser souls grasping for fashion have finally, after years, found a dim approximation of his original aesthetic insight, of my insight.

This is a kind of paper you see in many drawing rooms now, I see in many drawing rooms. Never quite so nice.

Not as good. But it is near enough, to the undiscerning eye – fools might look at this paper, this paper beneath my hands, and think of the paper on their own walls with satisfaction, in the belief that they themselves have approached a kind of a mark.

Although it could be cleaned, it is no longer *select*.

Tomorrow I will have it torn down, ripped away; I will choose anew.

There is a moment of panic. A thrill of fear. For I saw what was about me, clear-eyed, and then days passed, years, custom, habit, and I failed to see. I failed to see the years. Passing. This wallpaper, my wallpaper, the paper which lines my study, it now trembles on the cusp of the banal, the ordinary – and I have realized it only just in time. And I will grow older. And I will lose my faculties. And time will fog my head. And there will come a day when I will look around me and see that everything around me all the works of my hand and eye have been surpassed long ago, long ago, and I will realize that I myself was surpassed, long ago.

My hands pressed against the paper. Outside, in the passageway, a gabble of voices.

> *(We hear briefly, at greater volume, still through a wall, the scene between* **CHARLES** *and the* **OLD LADY**.*)*

Nevermind. Nevermind the gabble of voices.

> *(During* **PAUL**'*s monologue we are seeing the actors act the scene, but tho their lips move there is no sound. The light shifts and shimmers around the set in a new way.)*

> *(The scene concludes with the imp reveal.)*

STAGE MANAGER. Hold please.

DIRECTOR. Okay is this our lighting land for this scene?

LIGHTS. This is our lighting land.

DIRECTOR. Love it.

7.
SIX PACK

(Big whirr forward.)

*(The **DIRECTOR** is onstage, working with **EVA** and **BEN**; they are adjusting a blocking moment and also discussing the function and flow of the scene.)*

(Weird noises are happening at a low volume.)

AD. *(Plopping down next to him.)* Hey.

JAKE. Hey.

AD. Chip, thingie?

JAKE. I'm good man, thanks.

(Tiny pause.)

AD. I cannot stop eating these.

JAKE. Yeah.

AD. They're ad-icktive.

JAKE. Yeah that's why I don't even start.

AD. That's disciplined. That's totally disciplined.

JAKE. Naw it's…nah.

AD. I totally admire that. I totally totally admire that. Look at this:

I could put it right back in the bag. I mean, right? It's this tiny tiny chip. I outweigh this chip by, like, ten thousand times, right?

And I'm not even hungry. There is no instinctive imperative. I do not have to have this chip. I don't! But I'm going to.

(Crunch.)

I had the chip.

I simply don't have the willpower. I totally admire that you have the willpower.

JAKE. I have a trainer who's a real hardcase. I've kind of got his voice in my head at this point. So that really helps.

AD. You have a trainer?

JAKE. Yup.

AD. I mean of course. Like he's not just the guy at the gym he's your whole trainer?

JAKE. I'm *one* of his clients.

AD. But he's not just a guy you go to he actually has responsibility for your training.

JAKE. Yeah.

AD. That's his job.

JAKE. Yeah, he's good. He's an asshole, which helps me out a lot. I'll give you his name you want.

AD. Oh um. Yeah. Yeah. I don't think, but yeah maybe someday.

JAKE. He's really good. Here, let me fish his number out of my phone.

AD. Oh um thanks. Yeah.

JAKE. Yeah no problem. Make sure you mention my name just, he works on a referral only system that's all.

AD. Cool. Cool.

JAKE. Okay. You ready?

AD. Oh. Uh, oh let me get my phone.

(*Rustling and seat creaking as he gets up.*)

E3. I hated that episode. But it *moved* me.

ASM. Yup.

E3. I had an emotional response. And then I hated myself, for being such a sucker.

E2. I think if you cry it wins though.

E3. I didn't cry.

E2. Same thing. I think you have to respect if you're moved by it.

E3. Um…

E2. Otherwise you're setting up, like, an artificial mind/ body/spirit dichotomy.

E3. …what?

E2. I think if part of you loves something, and part of you hates something, the part of you that loves something wins. And is right.

E3. Okay first of all, dichotomy is *two*, right? Not three

ASM. Triotomy?

E2. Whatever the term is.

E3. You said mind/body/spirit which is three. Things going on at once. Our brain is divided into two halves so I don't think we can have a triple response to something.

E2. Well first of all I think that's just your brain talking.

E3. It…yes. Yes it is. What else is there to talk?

E2. What, indeed.

E3. What?

E2. That's what I'm saying. What I'm saying is that our brain is set up to dichotomize. But the world – because of its structure – but the *world* isn't structured into dichotomies. We just perceive it that way.

ASM. Okay but aren't we part of the world?

E3. Wait but putting, putting all of this aside just for the moment. What about my brain structure means that the dumb stupid sentimental part of me which is moved by a cheap emotional set up and some gooey music is right? Why is that part right, and the part of me which knows I'm just being *played* is wrong?

E2. I think we learn to be ashamed of things. And it's actually not that easy to move people. They just make it look easy, but it's not. I was trying to think the other day, I was thinking about how I don't think I've ever made anyone cry. In a *moved* kind of a way. Even accidentally being a jerk I don't think I've made anyone cry more than, like, once but I've definitely, I've definitely never *moved* anyone to tears.

E3. Huh.

(There is a silence.)

Me neither, come to think of it.

(A tiny silence.)

ASM. I did. Once.

E3. *Did* you. Who?

ASM. My dad. I told him – well he was dying of cancer and he was on a lot of meds so, he was sort of susceptible, I think. But I – yeah.

(Tiny pause.)

E3. Yeah. That counts.

JAKE. 917-434-1390

AD. 917-434-1390?

JAKE. Yup.

AD. Okay. Got it. Jake's *(As he types it in.)* trainer.

JAKE. His name is Ricky Cortinez.

AD. R…i…c…k…y C…o…r…t…i…n…e…z. Alright. Personal Trainer. You don't have a six pack or anything do you?

JAKE. I kind of do, actually, yeah. A *small* one not a major.

AD. A *six pack*.

JAKE. Like I said, he's a hard case.

AD. I am so not gay. Not that there is anything – I just want to state that, if I were gay, I would not ask you that because I would be concerned that you would… if I were a gay guy I'd be very chill, very low key, I'd probably be a lot, calmer…

JAKE. Not a problem man.

AD. Is that a lot of work, a six pack?

JAKE. *(For some reason this is the first time we hear discernable discomfort.)* It's a lot of work to get it, established. Not so much work to maintain. You know, you get into a rhythm. You ignore the chips.

AD. If I had one my problem is I'd be looking for excuses to whip it out all the time. I'd be, like, that guy who always happens to be removing his shirt. I'd be that guy. But your agent must know, right?

JAKE. *(Still uncomfortable.)* Uh, yeah. Yeah. My agent knows.

AD. Cool.

> *(Also in the house:)*

SIGET. Hey Beth should I have boobs for the bordello scene?

COSTUME. Oh – you don't need to.

SIGET. No but I mean, if I've got the corsetty thing anyway, it would be good to be kind of spilling out, right?

COSTUME. It's possible. Were you thinking just this one scene?

SIGET. I was but if that's too much to deal with in the quickchanges maybe all my characters could be stacked

Hey Eva just so you know I'm asking for bazoombas.

> *(The discussion on stage has recently concluded, and the* **DIRECTOR** *has stepped off into the house,* **BEN** *has shifted into the wings,* **EVA** *is still on stage.)*

EVA. Bazoombas?

SIGET. Bosoms. Bazoombas? That's right, right: Bazoombas?

EVA. Bazoooooombas – now I don't know. I can't tell!

COSTUME. I think bazoombas is right.

SIGET. Well I'm getting 'em. If you want to upgrade your firepower.

EVA. Oh. I guess I feel like. I'm fine aren't I? I feel like I'm fine

COSTUME. You are totally fine.

EVA. I mean *(Looking down at herself.) am* I fine?

COSTUME. You're totally fine.

EVA. Yeah but am I?

SIGET. You totally are. I just don't want you to feel taken unawares.

EVA. Maybe I should. *(To* **COSTUME**.*) Can* I?

SIGET. Oh do it. Do it.

EVA. Yes. I'm going to do it.

COSTUME. Don't go hog wild, those dresses are fitted.

SIGET. Elliott you don't mind if we're breastier do you?

DIRECTOR. *(In the house. Has been discussing something with* **LIGHTS**.*)* ...what??

SIGET. Boobier. Eva and me are going boobier for this you don't mind do you?

DIRECTOR. Oh my god. I didn't hear that question. I definitely didn't answer it. Beth?

COSTUME. It's fine with me.

EVA. It doesn't mess with your *mis en scène* or anything does it?

DIRECTOR. This is strictly between you girls. Women. Whatever Beth wants in the way of is fine with me.

EVA. We must, we must

SIGET & EVA. *(Chanting.)* We must increase our bust!

DIRECTOR. Dear Jesus

AD. *(In a confidential whisper.)* Should we ask Carla?

DIRECTOR. Carla?

AD. If this was part of her conception of those characters. That they uh...

DIRECTOR. No one is going outside the bounds of normal physiological structure, as far as I know.

AD. I know but isn't that, I'm just thinking –

DIRECTOR. Carla didn't say anything during auditions about breast size and character. I'm going to assume it's fine.

AD. I should put it in my notes though shouldn't I?

DIRECTOR. *(Micropause.)* Yes, by all means.

8.
WATER FEATURE

(Bit of a whirr.)

(The Forest is unveiled.)

(E2 is on a ladder, adjusting a bulb, his head not visible.)

STAGE MANAGER. Alright ladies and gentleman, we are back at places.

I want to thank everyone for maintaining focus thus far. We have four and a half hours to go until we end our day. And we have two more days to go in total. So I want to thank you, in advance, for *continuing* to maintain focus. Page 34, Ladies and Gentlemen, page 34.

EVA. *(In the house.)* Yay page 34!

DIRECTOR. *(General announcement.)* Let's see if we can bear down and finish this play in the next 40 minutes. If we can finish the play in the next 40 minutes we can all go home early, and take the next two and a half days off.

(BEN enters.)

Ben.

BEN. 10 4 chief.

STAGE MANAGER. Actors to the stage. Actors to the stage. Killing the mosquito. Actors to the stage.

DIRECTOR. Hey Ben?

BEN. Yeah

DIRECTOR. Will you muck your hair up a bit?

BEN. *(Hand to head.)* You want me to lose the part?

DIRECTOR. That's right.

BEN. You mean craziness?

DIRECTOR. No I think it should just look like it usually does.

BEN. You mean really cool and sexy.

DIRECTOR. *(A beat.)* That's right.

BEN. You don't mean for all of it you just mean for the forest scenes.

DIRECTOR. Just for the forest.

BEN. I'll see what I can do there's a lot of gel.

DIRECTOR. Beth we need his hair to have the power of variability.

COSTUME. Between the modern and the other scenes?

DIRECTOR. That's right.

COSTUME. That's great. And that's all very well and good. Right now we're defying the laws of physics just to get the costume changes in time.

STAGE MANAGER. Actors to the stage, ladies and gentlemen.

ASM. Molly, we can't find Jake.

STAGE MANAGER. He isn't down there?

ASM. He was here at half hour. But we can't find him now.

STAGE MANAGER. Did you look outside? Is he smoking?

E2. I looked outside.

STAGE MANAGER. Did you try his –

ASM. Not yet.

STAGE MANAGER. Alright, I will. Look – and he's not in the bathroom.

ASM. *(We're not amateurs.)* No.

> (**EVA** *has already appeared, also in modern dress, rather on trend.*)

DIRECTOR. Come on people, hup hup.

EVA. Hup hup.

> (*She does a brief march in place and then discards it.*)

SOUND. "hup hup." You don't hear that so much. In real life.

DIRECTOR. "hup-hup people, hup-hup" that's a leadership term. Phrase.

SOUND. What you need is a quirt.

DIRECTOR. That's right, I do need a quirt. Beth, you're going to need to provide me with a quirt.

COSTUME. With a quirt?

DIRECTOR. With a quirt.

COSTUME. A *quirt?*

(**SOUND** *laughs.*)

DIRECTOR. Yes, woman, with a quirt.

COSTUME. Quirt.

DIRECTOR. Quirt.

COSTUME. *(Trying to sound it out.)* Qwuu – spell it.

DIRECTOR. Q-u. I-r-t.

COSTUME. Q. U. I. R. T

DIRECTOR. You'll want to look it up.

COSTUME. I'm not going to look it up. I'm making an executive decision: no. There is enough nonsense in my life. I do not need to know about this ridiculous

(**SOUND** *laughs.*)

thing. This quirt thing. No. It's so clear to me that it's not actually important. Whatever the hell it is.

DIRECTOR. I'm ordering you. As your leader.

COSTUME. As my *leader.*

DIRECTOR. As your leader. I am *ordering* you to *know* what a quirt is.

COSTUME. Sorry, Elliott. I'm keepin' it sane.

AD. Quisling?

COSTUME. What was that?

AD. I hope you don't think I'm a quisling.

COSTUME. Oh…yeah. Right. No, I know that word.

AD. Qwa – luckily I can't think of any more.

COSTUME. *(Disinterested.)* I'm downstairs if anyone needs me.

LIGHTS. Listen, I'd really love to get started on this.

DIRECTOR. It's ten past, Richter. You're losing your grip.

STAGE MANAGER. We're missing Jake.

AD. Qwanza.

> *(Somewhere before this* **PAUL** *has already wandered up to the stage, in his pants, a clean and appropriately deluxe looking shirt, but not full costume.)*

DIRECTOR. *(Calling out – this is for effect, rather than meant to be effective.)* Jake! Jacob Holder, to the stage please. Jacob Holder, to the stage!

STAGE MANAGER. I'm just giving him a call now.

Jake this is Molly Richter we're at time. We need you up on the stage immediately, thank you.

SOUND. Oh hey there's a spill here. Major major spill.

STAGE MANAGER. Spill where.

SOUND. Right, over…

STAGE MANAGER. Alright, Jamie.

ASM. Yup!

STAGE MANAGER. Jamie we have a spill in the house.

SOUND. Looks like it's an entire water bottle upended.

STAGE MANAGER. Water.

SOUND. A big liter-y…

ASM. On my way.

STAGE MANAGER. Anything…

SOUND. *(Sticking his head down to look.)* No it's a very lucky little mini flood. Right down the aisle. Just damp.

LIGHTS. It's almost like a like a water feature.

> *(Sound of a channel switch.)*

SOUND. Oh hey, Erik, I found your exacto knife under a seat do you still care.

E2. No, I have a better one now.

SOUND. I'll put it on my table.

E2. *(Amiably.)* That one can rot in hell.

> *(Sound of a channel switch.)*

(From the back of the house:)

JAKE. Listen, I'm incredibly sorry.

DIRECTOR. Young Jake, there you are.

JAKE. I'm incredibly sorry. I was on a call and I absolutely lost track of time. My total apologies.

DIRECTOR. *(Pleasantly.)* Apology accepted and you can now hustle your butt up onto the stage if you will.

JAKE. Sorry Molly.

STAGE MANAGER. I need to remind you not to leave the theater in costume.

JAKE. *(Micropause.)* Of course. Right. I will be totally careful about that.

STAGE MANAGER. *(Apology accepted.)* Great.

PAUL. Jake. You've decided to join us.

JAKE. *(Generally.)* I'm really sorry everyone.

ASM. I'll be out of the aisle in one…sec.

PAUL. *(With great deliberation.)* Our box office bonanza has returned.

(Microbeat.)

E3. Guys. It's happening.

ASM. *(Under her breath.)* Yup.

E2. What's happening.

E3. You're going to want to get up here man.

JAKE. *(Evenly, a greeting:)* Hey Paul.

PAUL. Did you actually, 'absolutely' lose track of the time?

JAKE. I did.

PAUL. You don't lose track of the time. You are punctual to the moment. You are always two minutes early. *Punctilious.* Polite. Correct. And then, every now and then, you're on a phone call. You "lose track." You don't lose track. You know exactly what time it is. You employ a calculus. That these extra ten minutes, with a high power personage in Los Angeles – I'm just guessing, here – are more pressing than ten minutes in this room, more valuable. Or please forgive me. Does any of this matter when your apologies are, as you say, "total."

E3. *Shit!*

STAGE MANAGER. Paul you're not actually onstage for this scene.

PAUL. I'm not, I'm offstage, where I am able to give it my full attention. In all of its vague and sloppy glory. If 'glory' is the word I most want to use. Which actually it isn't.

DIRECTOR. Paul.

> (**BEN**, *who was onstage, has slowly edged off of it by this point.*)

PAUL. Eva, Siget, no offence. You are both actors for whom I have a real regard. Siget is a more serious and committed performer but Eva although you generally insist on squandering it you have a real talent, and some fine instincts.

DIRECTOR. *(Very firm, very fierce.)* Paul that's enough.

STAGE MANAGER. Paul I'm going to have to ask you to step off the stage so that we can continue working on this scene.

PAUL. *You haven't earned a place at this table, son.*

> (**EVA** *erupts into a fury.*)

EVA. God*dammit* Paul you fucking *ruiner* I can't *stand* it

Do you know what it was I didn't say? When you asked me – which is *such* bullshit – *such* bullshit – "don't you ever remember what it was like when I touched you" – *which what, what, what what <u>controlly</u> bullshit* – and I said no *to be polite* because the *truth* – which you are so *very* fond of – the *truth* is that yes I do think about it, I do think about it *every single day*. Since now I have to see you *every single day*. And every single day I look at you, and I do remember you touching me, and I *shudder*. You fucking, fucking, *ruiner*.

> *(She storms off.)*

(There is an amazing ghastly silence. Everything has stopped. All is still.)

(Very quiet. As if they can be heard. Which they can't:)

<u>**E2**</u>. Wow.

<u>**E3**</u>. Yup.

<u>**E2**</u>. Wow.

> (**PAUL** *walks out of the theater through the auditorium.)*

> *(We hear the street door open and close.)*

> *(There is still a silence.)*

> *(Finally:)*

DIRECTOR. Richter, why don't we call a ten minute.

> *(Microbeat.)*

STAGE MANAGER. Ten minutes everyone, ten minutes.

DIRECTOR. Young Jacob, a word with you, if I may.

Richter I'll need two of your cigarettes.

STAGE MANAGER. Sure.

> *(Purse fumbling.)*

DIRECTOR. You smoke?

JAKE. I don't, no.

DIRECTOR. But you can. You know how to do it.

JAKE. I do.

DIRECTOR. I gave it up twelve years ago. Let's step outside and have a smoke. Thank you Richter.

STAGE MANAGER. And you'll need this.

DIRECTOR. So we will.

> *(Fires up a lighter.)*

STAGE MANAGER. *(Kind of on automatic.) Not* in here

> *(He clicks it shut.)*

DIRECTOR. *(Also slightly on automatic.)* No fire. No darkness. This is the malady of the American Theater.

And let's make it a fifteen.

STAGE MANAGER. *Fifteen* minutes everyone. *Fifteen.*

AD. *(Trying to be a positive part of normalizing the situation.)* Thank you fifteen.

> *(There a break which is an intermission.)*

> *(Stage lights out, house lights up at full.)*

STAGE MANAGER. *(Her voice comes, not from her speaker, but from the general sound system.)* Ladies and gentlemen this is our fifteen minute break. Please be back promptly in fifteen minutes. Fifteen minutes ladies and gentlemen, fifteen minutes.

9.
GODDESSES

(A whirr forward with a certain tenor to it.)

*(***SIGET*** is lying in the pink room, stretching out and singing a rambly series of variants on goddesses/swine.)*

E3. Guys I want to warn you. If you were thinking of going outside. It's still light out there.

ASM. "it burns it burns"

E2. Yeah that's why I bring my dinner.

E3. And dinner is?

E2. Tonight dinner is a horrible microwave deep dish pizza from the deli on the corner.

E3. Right right. It's true. Sometimes the goal is just to stay alive.

*(***SIGET*** hits a particular rhythmic bit of repetition:)*

SIGET. Goddesses, goddesses, never seen with swine

Goddesses, goddesses, never seen with swine

*(Which the ***E'S*** pick up on and one and then all start humming along.)*

SIGET, E2, E3, ASM.
GODDESSES, GODDESSES, NEVER SEEN WITH SWINE
GODDESSES, GODDESSES, NEVER SEEN WITH SWINE

(And are sort of bummed when she, all unaware, swaps out rhythms and launches into a kind of R&B trill where she cannot be followed.)

(They continue on for two beats of:)

GODDESSES, GODDESSES, NEVER SEEN WITH SWINE
GODDESSES, GODDESSES, NEVER SEEN WITH SWINE

(But can't hold it against her contrary musics.)

ASM. *(Speculative but firm.)*
IST EINE HUNST DIE FAR DIE FLABBERGAST

IST SWEINHUNST DIE FI HEIN HEINST.
IST EINE HUNST DIE FAR DIE FLABBERGAST
IST SWEINHUNST DIE FI HEIN HEINST.

E3. *(Impressed.)* Whoa

E2. *(Trying it.)* Ist eine hunst die…

ASM. *(Slowish, educational, partly singing:)* Ist eine hunst die far die Flabbergast

E2 & E3. Ist eine hunst die far die Flabbergast

ASM. Ist Sweinhunst die fi hein heinst.

E2 & E3. Ist Sweinhunst die fi hein heinst.

> *(Briefly they trill along to "Flabbergast" to the tune* **SIGET** *is currently adopting for "Goddesses.")*

STAGE MANAGER. *(On the overhead mic.)* Alright folks we are back from dinner, we are back from dinner. This is half hour. Please be on stage in costume in a half hour. Half hour folks, half an hour.

10.
DYING INSIDE

(A brief jump forward.)

(There is a chair. And a side table with a book.)

(EVA enters.)

(She goes to the chair and picks up a shawl which she's left dangling from it. Wraps it around her shoulders.)

(She looks…)

EVA. Is that how downstage it's going to be?

STAGE MANAGER. It's on the mark.

EVA. Is that really how downstage we had it in the rehearsal room?

STAGE MANAGER. Should be.

DIRECTOR. Problem, Eva?

EVA. I just thought…it seems really far. It seems strange that I would, see it. It feels like it's out of my peripheral.

STAGE MANAGER. *(Patient.)* That's where it's been.

EVA. Really?

STAGE MANAGER. If you want I can remeasure.

EVA. No. But do you think we could move it.

DIRECTOR. *(Delicate.)* Tell what Eva why don't you shift it where you want it and we'll see.

(She looks at the table. Looks around the room. Looks back at the chair. Concentrating very hard.)

(She walks over to the table, and moves it centerstage a scooch more than a foot.)

(She walks back to the chair. She stands by the chair, pantomimes removing her shawl, turning, seeing the table.)

EVA. Could we have it there?

DIRECTOR. Julie?

LIGHTS. Works for me.

> (**JAMIE** *comes up onto the stage and carefully re-marks the new marks and carefully removes the old marks.*)

LIGHTS. Alright Tim we're going to sort this out during the break – for the moment just release everything.

DIRECTOR. We all good?

STAGE MANAGER. One moment.

Alright, from top of scene please.

> (*There is a chair. And a side table with a book.*)
>
> (**EVA** *enters.*)
>
> (*She goes to the chair and picks up a shawl, which she's left dangling from it. Wraps it around her shoulders.*)
>
> (*She looks…she sees the book.*)
>
> (*She looks around. She goes to the book.*)
>
> (*She removes a letter, examines it briefly, begins to read from it:*)
>
> (*She reads from it for a while. She looks at another letter, starts to read.*)

EVA. "My dear, dearest Charles. You ask about my person. I am considerably tanner. And there are some marks, on my back. I was lashed for insubordination. Do you remember what that is to be lashed for insubordination, not since we were caned as boys. I wanted to know what it is, to be lashed for insubordination, as a man. I wanted to know what that physical injury is. What that humiliation is. So I was insubordinate. The mate knew it was deliberate, calculated, the whole crew knew. He gave me such a look. But it was a provocation and he could not let it pass. I was ringed on the foredeck by a circle of uneasy men in the high hot noon, and he whipped me. It is a mark, and I will carry it for a while,

but I do not suppose that it will be a scar so do not
know if it will remain when I see you next. It may be
that you will never see it."

(Another letter:)

"I lashed a man. I said to the mate let me do it. He
said you will spare him – he was a man I was friendly
with – so the mate supposed I meant to do it to go easy
on him. I said no, I've watched you beat men, I'll go no
harder, I'll go no softer, you can watch me, and you can
step in if it isn't so. I wanted to know what it is. But like
the time I took my own lashing, it's impossible to know
what the thing really is, if you choose it. Our heart is
made from our choices, but our life is made from that
which we cannot choose. The man I lashed wouldn't
look me in the eye again, though he would have had
that same injury if I had done it or no."

(Another letter:)

"You have me thinking about my body. I've been
looking at my gut. It's a solid gut, not a jelly one, and I
don't mind it. It's a man's accumulation of matter. I'm
proud of it even, in a way, but then I will see a tawny boy,
nineteen, twenty-two, stripped to the waist to clamber
the rigging or swab the deck all muscle and taut flesh
and I remember that that was what I was, and that I used
to think there was a real virtue in that – it wasn't vanity,
it was the value of nothing extra, clean and strong and
trim, like a sail. My body isn't what I used to believe in
and, if I'm honest, it's not what I believe in now."

So are we really *not* cutting that last letter? I mean,
I will do it, if I have to do it, but I thought maybe we
were cutting it?

STAGE MANAGER. We're doing the letter.

DIRECTOR. As far as I know Carla is still on the fence on
the letter.

EVA. It's a great letter. It's a perfectly great letter. I'm happy
to say it. It's just that when I say the letter after saying

all the other letters I feel – in advance, I know – I feel
the audience die quietly inside.

STAGE MANAGER. Moving on.

DIRECTOR. Noted. Moving on.

EVA. Right. Moving on.

11.
WAS A CLASS

(Big chunk forward.)

(All of this is while **PAUL** *and the* **DIRECTOR** *are sitting towards the very back of the stage having a discussion chairs turned upstage which we can't hear or even really make out their faces.)*

(There's lights tinkering and low, basically unintelligible lighting language.)

*(***JAKE*** and ***BEN*** are in the back of the house, talking, their voices pitched low.)*

JAKE. The first time I saw Paul, I mean, in the flesh, I was in a Richard Foreman show. I was a dwarf.

BEN. You were in a Richard Foreman show?

JAKE. I was a dwarf.

BEN. I thought you got sucked straight into L.A.

This was seven, eight years ago. Fresh out of college. A dwarf, and very excited to be a dwarf.

I mean I couldn't believe it. That was beyond my goal, at the time. I had exceeded my dreams of glory.

And I was onstage one night and I saw Paul in the audience. Like five feet away or something. It freaked my shit out. Because I had *studied* him. In school.

Paul?

JAKE. Yeah I had a teacher who I guess, in retrospect, was pretty hip. I mean I didn't know. All I knew was, he was being presented to me as a kind of, as a total member of the *canon.*

BEN. *What* was this class?

JAKE. It was called Downtown Theater NYC.

BEN. Was a class.

JAKE. Bennington.

BEN. Oh, yeah. Sure.

JAKE. So I'm onstage. I see him. I literally don't even remember what happened next all I know is that I exerted myself to my utmost to be the very best dwarf conceivable. I went into intricate mental and emotional places. Afterwards I turn to one of the other dwarfs I'm like breathless I'm like: how was I? How was I? She looked at me she was like, you were fine, man, you were fine.

I saw him in everything I could see him in.

I wanted to do theatRE again anyway but. When they said. I was like: this is heaven.

(Smallish pause.)

Probably I should have said something to him. But I was shy.

(Longish pause.)

BEN. Yeah. That might have helped.

(Long beat.)

The first time I saw him perform I was seeing some show at Nada which is long gone it was this low ceilinged, dive theater I guess, on the Lower East Side, kind of dank

JAKE. Yeah I know *Nada.*

BEN. *(Slightly startled.)* This is long before your time

JAKE. I know *of* it.

BEN. From the *class?*

JAKE. Nah, I think just from around. When I got here. It was a legend.

BEN. A *legend.*

JAKE. History. It was history. A lot of people were like: "Nada."

ASM. *(Even sottoer voce.)* Ben?

BEN. *(Ditto.)* Yah?

ASM. Sorry to interrupt, but you were looking for your script?

BEN. Oh okay, great. Thank you.

ASM. *(A very polite 'yup.')* Yup

> *(A small recombobulating beat.)*

BEN. History.

That's hilarious. It was cheap. It was extra cheap. Cheaper than…well, than other spaces which are also gone now.

JAKE. When people talked about the '90s.

BEN. Right. The Historical '90s. Well it was dirty – a lot of people really loved it. I never loved it that low ceiling. I think that's hard. Intrinsically hard. An extra high ceiling is hard too. The Ohio could be hard – the Ohio –

JAKE. Yeah that was my time.

BEN. Right. Of course. I forget.

> *(A particularly bright cue has landed on* **PAUL** *and the* **DIRECTOR**. *The* **DIRECTOR** *turns slightly, squinting a bit, and raises his hand to dismiss the cue. From this point on the light tinkering is subdued and takes places in parts of the stage away from them.)*

JAKE. But that was when you first saw him.

BEN. *(Simply.)* Sure.

I'd just been in the city a few months. I applied to a conservatory training program. I was going to be a Shakespearian actor. But I didn't get in. So I moved to New York because I didn't know what else to do and I met people and they said oh, you have to go see this show. And I went to go see it. And I didn't know what it…was. I had literally never seen anything like that. I had no concept how or where or why it would ever *occur* to anyone to *do* that. I was profoundly puzzled. And in the middle of all of it was this *person*. Paul.

And I didn't see him in anything else until six months later. In another tiny place. And I thought: huh.

And the third time I saw him, I don't even remember what it was he was in, it was so terrible, but something clicked and I thought I Want To Work With This Person. It was like I shook my fist towards the heavens. And I had this goal. I didn't reapply to the conservatory.

And three years later I was cast in a play with him. I couldn't get up my nerve for two weeks. Finally we were at drinks after and I said you know…and he couldn't have been nicer about it. And he really made a point to, to be encouraging. Which meant the *world* to me.

I had an offer. This was a year later, a year and a half later I had a very strong offer to come out to LA and it wasn't…for sure…but they wanted to look at me for this pilot and it would have been a very big commitment if it were picked up. And I didn't love…the role. I didn't love the script. I mean I didn't like it at all. But there were big names and it was a *lot* of money and I thought I should go out there, right? Of course. Of course you go out there of course and I was…troubled about it and I ran into him, literally, on the street and I said we were friendly we weren't friends but we ran into each other on the street, chatted for two minutes, and I said please can I buy you a drink and we it was almost sort of hilarious we rotated in place and right behind us was a bar, a fake Irish Pub, and we walked in and we talked for hours and hours.

And then I called my agent and I said no.

JAKE. Did the show get picked up?

     (A pausey beat.)

BEN. Yes.

You know it. It's still running.

Literally I can't bear to say the name.

It's not a great show, it's really not.

Half of the time I think: if I had said yes, I would always wonder what would have happened if I'd said no. I'd be one of those people who says I have all the money in the world and yet I have given away that which is priceless: my honor. As an artist.

(Small pause.)

JAKE. Is that a quote?

BEN. No.

The other half of the time I indulge in Net Worth Porn.

It wasn't a solid offer.

I imagine this is something you struggle with yourself, from the other end of it.

(Bit of a pause.)

JAKE. *(Delicate.)* I've actually been, very lucky. In the projects I've been involved in.

BEN. Right. Of course.

12.
THE RIGHT SHIRT

(In the forest. In the Dark.)

(Three imps have crept onto the stage and are moving forward with intent. We can see nothing of them, but their long glow-in-the-dark finger-claws and possibly some sort of glow-in-the-dark imp face largely hooded.)

(The sounds of a jungle at night,)

LIGHTS. Can we hold a moment?

STAGE MANAGER. Hold please.

(The imps go slack.)

LIGHTS. That was late on 254.

STAGE MANAGER. Was late.

LIGHTS. It needs to be bum bada bum bum bada bum, bum bum bum – you call it here – bum bada bada – and here it needs to be completed.

STAGE MANAGER. Okay. Wait. So it's – bum baba bum bum bada bum, bum – wait. I'm just going to run

Standbye Sound 63. Sound 63 – go.

(We hear the music. The imps joggle a bit with the music.)

LIGHTS. *(Along with that bit.)* bum bada bum bum bada bum, bum bum bum – and that's where you need to have called it

STAGE MANAGER. Hold.

bum bada bum bum bada bum, bum bum bum – okay. Okay.

LIGHTS. Shall we run through it again?

STAGE MANAGER. Imps, will you please retract? We are going to run this again from the start.

(The imps retract.)

STAGE MANAGER. Ready backstage?

ASM. Ready.

E2. Ready.

STAGE MANAGER. Standby Lights 252 & 253.

Standby Sound cues 62 & 63

Lights 252 & Sound 62 – go.

Lights 253 & Sound 63 – go.

(The imps re-creep.)

(The moment.)

(The moment passes.)

LIGHTS. Let's hold.

(Microbeat.)

STAGE MANAGER. Hold please.

LIGHTS. bum bada bum bum bada bum, bum bum **bum**

bum bada bum bum bada bum, bum bum **bum**

STAGE MANAGER. bum bada bum bum bada bum, bum bum bum. Okay. I'm going to look at this additionally on my break.

LIGHTS. Why don't we run through it again.

STAGE MANAGER. This? I don't know that this at this point is the best use of our time.

(A beat or two.)

LIGHTS. If I'm going to cut the cue it's simpler to just do it now.

STAGE MANAGER. Why don't I take a look at it on my break.

LIGHTS. It's a hat on a hat. Anyway. Honestly. Why don't I just cut it. *(To assist.)* Cue 254 delete – enter.

(Beat.)

(Beat.)

(Beat.)

(Beat.)

STAGE MANAGER. Imps? We're going to take it again from your entrance. Sleepers. Please reset.

> *(The imps return offstage.)*

> *(In the holding moments, the imps – prompted by the initial experiments of one among them – have been exploring their glow-in-the-dark fingers: perhaps wriggling them in an aquatic manner; perhaps exploiting their usefulness as puppets; perhaps engaging in the preliminary stages of hand-combat.)*

> *(As the scene is running again:)*

E3. How's it going back there?

ASM. Seems to be going... Erik?

E2. Uh huh.

ASM. He's right there, right?

E2. Uh huh.

E3. So you can't say anything

E2. Uh uh.

E3. But he's there

E2. Uh huh.

E3. How's he seem?

E2. *(Cautiously but not totally optimistic.)* Eh.

ASM. He's wearing the right shirt.

E3. Can he hear you?

ASM. No.

E3. I mean Erik.

E2. Uh huh.

E3. I mean, is he *listening*.

E2. *(The tonal resister for 'I don't know' with uncertainty on the 'know.')* Mmmm...huhuhhuh

E3. Because you sound really cagey. Probably if you just said words, outright, it would be better; you sound super secretive.

E2. *(Brief exasperated intonement.)*

E3. No I'm serious, if you sound casual you can probably say almost anything and no one will notice.

ASM. He's asked, he's asked us – I mean, *before* – to stay off headsets if we can. When he's waiting to go on. It hurts his concentration.

E3. Jesus Christ. Run the show with telepathy guys, please.

ASM. In a nice way. He asked in a nice way. To refrain. If it's not absolutely necessary.

E3. I can barely hear you.

ASM. Aren't you supposed to be paying attention to something or something?

E3. Chill guys just, chill.

> *(The imps are just reaching their goal and there is a vast amplified gasp; they retract in a super hasty scramble as…)*

> *(Lights up on the sleepers:* **EVA** *and* **JAKE**, *in modern clothing, sprawled on a blanket, picnic basket nearby.* **EVA** *has gasped awake and is looking around wildly, sensing something,* **JAKE** *is only just roused and looks about with confusion.)*

13.
UNLUCKY THIRTEEN

(A gay but tawdry Victorian bordello.)

(CHARLES *is bouncing* **LUCILLE** *[***SIGET***] – in red and white frills – on his lap.)*

CHARLES. Lucille. You are a marvelously ginger girl, Lucille. She is, isn't she?

CARSTAIRS. She's got a lot going on.

CHARLES. And what I'm going to do with *you*. I'm going to tickle you, on the belly.

LUCILLE. Oh now.

CHARLES. And I'm going to rumple your skirt.

LUCILLE. Whee!

CHARLES. And I'm going to take you upstairs. All the way up those stairs, and what do you think about that?

CARSTAIRS. She isn't six, Charles.

LUCILLE. I think it's splendid. But first, before you do, will you buy me one more of those drinks with the fizz in them? I'm so terribly thirsty. Then, I can't wait!

CHARLES. Can't wait, no. Of course you can't! One more of those very expensive fizzy drinks, coming up.

　　　　*(***CHARLES*** *exits.)*

LUCILLE. And how come you're sitting here all by your lonesome?

CARSTAIRS. I'm not at all alone.

LUCILLE. 'Course you aren't. I'm right here, ain't I?

　　　　(She plops next to him.)

CARSTAIRS. Technically speaking you aren't here at all; you're there.

　　　　(Points to where she was.)

LUCILLE. Not anymore I'm not.

CARSTAIRS. Well you're going to have to move back when he returns.

LUCILLE. What if we was to slip upstairs right now. We'd be over and done by the time he returns; those fizzy drinks is laborious.

CARSTAIRS. Over and done? Madam, my pride!

LUCILLE. No then?

CARSTAIRS. No.

> *(Over the last four lines of this:)*

LIGHTS. Richter we're going to need to replace a lamp

STAGE MANAGER. Now? Do we really have to?

LIGHTS. We really have to.

> *(There's been something funky and sinister and dim with the lights.)*

STAGE MANAGER. Ladies and gentlemen hold please, while we replace a lamp.

> *(PAUL stands, abruptly, exits the stage as E2 is entering with a ladder and bulb.)*

STAGE MANAGER. We should be underway again momentarily.

STAGE MANAGER. Jamie is he heading towards the dressing rooms?

> *(Pause.)*

ASM. Just the bathroom I think.

DIRECTOR. *(This is an only partially rhetorical question.)* How hopelessly behind are we?

STAGE MANAGER. Well...fairly.

DIRECTOR. More than normal.

STAGE MANAGER. Yes. Quite a bit more than normal.

DIRECTOR. Brilliant. I relish the challenge. I embrace this opportunity to excel. I accept the vast...self improvement which is going to wash over me in a mist of perfection because I had the spine, and the spleen, to progress forward against horrible obstacles instead of doing what a sane person would do which is to chuck this all and go home and get into bed and sleep for five days and then apply to law school.

STAGE MANAGER. What are the chances we open this do you think?

DIRECTOR. *(A considering pause.)* 50/50?

You know I took the LSAT five years ago. Just on a whim. My scores were pretty good.

STAGE MANAGER. Five years ago it probably wasn't too late to go.

> *(**BEN** has come out on stage and he and **SIGET** are chatting. She has not raised her voice but suddenly we hear her:)*

SIGET. I did a show at HERE years and years ago, back when it was HOME, where a mouse wandered onstage during a performance and then it died.

I saw it happen and then I was supposed to have the big part of my scene, right next to the dead mouse

so I changed the blocking of the scene so that I was playing it, really anywhere I could find light that was anywhere else

my scene partner hadn't seen any of this he had no idea what was going on

afterwards he was really pissed – he was that kind of actor anyway, kind of paranoid all the time about were you going to undermine him and he got really angry and he was like, that was really unprofessional, you were really pulling focus in that scene

I said yes I was pulling focus. Away from the dead mouse!

> *(In the house:)*

EVA. *(Low voice.)* Hey Molly?

STAGE MANAGER. Yes Eva.

EVA. *(Continuing in a low almost whisper.)* I know this really isn't great timing. But I got a call from my agent.

STAGE MANAGER. Uh huh.

EVA. And she really, really wants me to go in for this audition. For that Soderberg series.

STAGE MANAGER. Uh huh.

EVA. And they want to see me today.

STAGE MANAGER. Ah hah.

EVA. They would also want that character to continue forward for at least a few episodes. My agent says that they were hinting that there's a possibility, that they might make the character a series regular, next season. She's basically a Girl but, she has a secret.

STAGE MANAGER. Eva we're very very behind.

EVA. I know but since we've been working out of sequence anyway…

STAGE MANAGER. Now that Paul's back in the room we're going through the script in order.

EVA. If Paul hadn't taken off yesterday there'd be that whole section I'm not in today…right?

>   (*A pause.*)

STAGE MANAGER. When would they shoot it?

EVA. Oh. (*Lying.*) Not until the run is finished. (*Beat.*) I'm not going to get it. But. I think if I don't go in for the audition my agent will go ballistic.

>   (*Small pause.*)

STAGE MANAGER. Let me see what I can work out.

EVA. Great! Thank you, Molly.

>   (*The bulb has been replaced.*)

>   (**PAUL** *has returned to the stage.*)

STAGE MANAGER. Alright we're back everyone. We're back. We're taking it from:

>   (**BEN** *leaves the stage.*)

STAGE MANAGER. Where do you want to take it from?

LIGHTS. From Charles' exit.

STAGE MANAGER. From Charles' exit. Lonesome.

*(*BEN *returns to the stage. And then realizes he isn't needed and retreats offstage again.)*

LUCILLE. And how come you're sitting here all by your lonesome?

CARSTAIRS. I'm not at all alone.

LUCILLE. 'Course you aren't. I'm right here, ain't I?

(She plops next to him.)

CARSTAIRS. Technically speaking you aren't here at all; you're there.

(Points to where she was.)

LUCILLE. Not any more I'm not.

CARSTAIRS. Well you're going to have to move back when he returns.

LUCILLE. What if we was to slip upstairs right now. We'd be over and done by the time he returns those fizzy drinks is laborious.

CARSTAIRS. Over and done? Madam, my pride!

LUCILLE. No then?

CARSTAIRS. No.

LUCILLE. You a poof too then, like him?

CARSTAIRS. A poof. What makes you think Charles is a poof. He's here, isn't he.

LUCILLE. I know one, don't I? Who better. They're steady trade but the girls doesn't like 'em. More in half the time they can't make a go of it.

CARSTAIRS. I would think you'd find that a relief.

LUCILLE. It's a *lot* of effort. And they're likely to weep. Besides, a girl has her pride.

CARSTAIRS. Well I can assure you, that Charles isn't a poof.

LUCILLE. Suit yerself. I suppose you don't like whores then.

CARSTAIRS. Madam, I adore them. But I'm afraid that I have very expensive tastes.

LUCILLE. *(Without rancor.)* an' I don't suit 'em.

CARSTAIRS. To your credit. Your sins are simple and easy ones, a child could commit any of them, and any competent priest could absolve them in a moment. The women I crave are depraved; I don't mean physically, although if I told you what they are capable of you would blush; they are deeply skilled and accomplished liars, supremely adept flatterers – *of themselves, most of all;* they have exquisite control of the heart muscle and can feign any emotion to perfection. Musical voices. Musical talents. And wonderful minds. Wonderful, terrible minds.

LUCILLE. They sound exhausting, those women.

(He throws his head back and laughs.)

The fellows who come here want a bit of a change, a bit of a laugh. I'm very popular because of my conversation; chatty. I can't play any music but I can sing something wonderful.

CARSTAIRS. Can you Lucille.

LUCILLE. Oh I can indeed.

CARSTAIRS. Extemporaire, or do you require the piano?

LUCILLE. Oh I don't need all of that. I can throw my head back and sing anywhere. Shall I right now?

CARSTAIRS. Yes. Please do.

LUCILLE.
    A GENTLEMAN LATTERLY OF MY ACQUAINTANCE
    FLATTERED ME WITH COMPLIMENTS DIVINE
    HE SAID MY LOOKS WOULD SUIT A GRECIAN GODDESS
    I SAID GODDESSES WERE NEVER SEEN WITH SWINE!

CARSTAIRS. Oh, Charles! There you are. Madam I am so sorry to interrupt such a performance, do you know what the Italians say? They say *Brava, Brava.* But you must be parched, and here, here is your drink!

(She takes a speculative sip.)

LUCILLE. Mickey has stinted me on the gin again. I must have a word with him. I am entitled to my portion, when a gentleman buys it me.

(She exits.)

CARSTAIRS. You know, Charles, you don't need to go through with this.

CHARLES. Through with what? Oh, with Lucille? You aren't bored are you Carstairs?

CARSTAIRS. Not one bit. It's not often that I'm so entertained at such a breakneck pace. But really, wouldn't you much rather go to the club and sit back with a glass of port?

CHARLES. I don't think Lucille is a bit tasteless Carstairs. I think she's a perfect example of her own sort; she would be tasteless if she aspired to be any more genteel. She's a bouncy girl and that's how I like 'em; it's not an appetite I am proud of but it is mine and, like many men, I'm prey to my own appetite even if my reason, or my friends, do not approve it. I'm raring to go Carstairs, not to put too fine a point upon it, rarin' to go! Drink has probably made me injudicious in my talk but there you have it.

CARSTAIRS. Charles.

CHARLES. What, Carstairs.

CARSTAIRS. This is a brief life, Charles. Tomorrow crowds forward, and then overcomes us.

CHARLES. It…tomorrow whatsit?

CARSTAIRS. Nothing. Here she comes.

LUCILLE. Darlin' – you doesn't mind if I call you that now do you. Mickey says, that there's the proper amount of gin in my drink for a weak one which is what he says you paid for. Do the right thing by a gel won't you? If a drink doesn't make your eyes cross when you first sip at it then it isn't festive, that's what I say. Come along won't you? Or would you rather talk with your fuddy duddy old friend there than with me? Come along I say.

CARSTAIRS. Go along, Charles. Unless drink has made you more than injudicious. Unless it has made you candid.

CHARLES. What's that you say there.

CARSTAIRS. Unless it has made you know your own heart. Charles, *look me in the eye.*

CHARLES. I'm sorry, Carstairs. You're simply speaking in riddles tonight.

STAGE MANAGER. Lights 305 – Go

(*Lights start to dim.*)

PAUL. I wonder, Ben, if we shouldn't rethink this exchange

STAGE MANAGER. Hold.

(*Lights return.*)

PAUL. Elliott, I'm sorry, do you mind if we take just a moment with this?

(*Micropause.*)

DIRECTOR. What did you have in mind?

PAUL. Because I don't, right now I just don't understand the scene, as played.

(*Micropause.*)

STAGE MANAGER. Kill the monitors downstairs.

DIRECTOR. Paul I thought we had, on Thursday, I thought we had reached a...

PAUL. We've talked a lot about tortured Victorian sensibilities. We've talked a lot about 'not-knowing'; I know Carla is very interested in the idea that this is a time where one can not-know, something I find academic and naïve, as I have stated.

(*Micropause.*)

DIRECTOR. I think that, uh, even in our own time, it's entirely possible to um. To be motivated by...internal forces...which we don't understand, and which we can't recognize.

PAUL. Of course. Yes, obviously. I expressed myself badly, I think, when we discussed it on Thursday. We don't know who the hell we are. Obviously. But in this particular scene, *as it is written*, given the parameters of character – *as written* –

and Ben, I must of course apologize, this is not a criticism of your work which is, as always, well considered and detailed, I'm trying to apply myself to the *dramaturgy* of this scene:

Frederick Carstairs is a man, is a character, is a man

And if he's plausible… I don't know. I suppose he is. I don't run in those circles. But I have found a way to believe him so.

who does not traffic in futility. We see him, in this scene, repeatedly, attempt to engage Charles on the topic of his motivations, his real appetites.

would Carstairs do, would he so exert himself if Charles was not as Tony Kushner says – albeit in a rather different context – on the threshold of revelation. What is this scene *about* is it *about* a

man who does not know himself who cannot accept his own sexuality – which is, in this day and age, a well worn topic – or is it about a man *on the verge* of knowing himself

in other words: does Carstairs apply himself to Charles because he is an intelligent – a terribly intelligent, if we are to believe the evidence of the script – man who understands that here is a real opportunity to bring Charles to a productive self understanding –

Or is Charles merely a fool, and Carstairs merely a foil.

> *(There is a sort of silence.)*

DIRECTOR. *(Holding his hand up.)* Let me just…

> *(**BEN** looks like he might be about to say something.)*

PAUL. Does Carstairs see accurately, or is the play ridiculous. Am I speaking, in this scene, am I speaking with a man who is oblivious or am I speaking with a man who is desperately trying to look out of his own eyes

Desperately…his eyes burning through the cage of his face

Trying, some essential part of his soul trying

To make communication

Again, Ben, this is not a criticism of your performance. I am only asking: *what are we doing here.*

Does Carstairs perform an essential function in this scene or is he merely forwarding the current of the plot. In life, we are all vital. Must we not be so in the theater?

> *(**DIRECTOR** has come onstage? **AD** hovering nearby?)*

DIRECTOR. I think that, um. I think that everything you say is insightful. I think that it is very relevant to the text, to the *subtext*, of the text I think this is a real part of… how the play operates I think that, in terms of how it is expressed, in this scene, in terms of the balance of self awareness, and insight, and subterranean motive –

PAUL. You want us to shove it under the rug.

DIRECTOR. I want those choices to inform the scene. But to remain inexplicit.

PAUL. Because you believe, in your…heart. Gut. That that is the richest choice. Or because that is the way Carla would have it.

> *(Micropause.)*

DIRECTOR. I think that in terms of the overall balance of the play that yes, that Carla's interpretation of this scene, is a sensible one. Or at any rate…a practical one.

PAUL. But you share my feeling that there is a more evocative truth.

DIRECTOR. I think our challenge, at this moment, is to work with the tools we have at hand.

PAUL. I do new plays because I love work which has only just emerged from the present moment.

But and I mean this with no malice whatsoever I wish all playwrights would die immediately after writing their script, so that they could be dead playwrights.

The person who writes the play is not the same person who sits in the rehearsal struggling to understand it through the limitations of their own insipid personality.

I treasure the art, but so often the artist doesn't have the courage of the art.

DIRECTOR. I think, ah. I think that that's, a fascinating question, um. The question of intention. I think that Carstairs, I wonder about if a fruitful way of looking at it is that Carstairs –

PAUL. What if, instead of ending the scene with one of Carla's – wonderful playwright in general, obviously, which is why I took this project – with one of Carla's habitual and unfortunate pretentious 'button' endings. What if the scene continues.

DIRECTOR. …if it continues?

PAUL. We can improvise, for the moment. Carla could take a look when she returns. If the new direction meets with her approval she could use our work as an inspiration or even a guideline towards a new scene. I'm happy to allow her to incorporate whatever of my language may seem fitting. I'm obviously not talking about a total rewrite just a continuation of the thought which will allow her to exploit the rich vein of inquiry which she herself originated. Perhaps, two or three pages at most. On the outside: four.

(A complex and in many ways ghastly pause.)

DIRECTOR. *(Gently. Reluctantly. Fearfully; his rope has ended.)* Paul. This is tech.

PAUL. I know it is. I know it is. We don't have the time. We don't have the strength. But this ship is foundering. Do we allow ourselves to sink, and to drown, only because the effort appears too great? Yes, it is a terrifying idea – this is supposed to be the home stretch – and I don't propose it lightly and I know we risk damage, insuperable damage to the production and believe me, that thought fills *me* with terror too, but I'm even *more* terrified at the damage to my soul, to all of our souls, to the souls of the audience which will give itself trustingly to us – do we face their need with cynicism, do we shrink away from this moment, this pivotal moment, and the very real bravery required to face the situation for what it is and more than to face it, to change it. *Change* it. What I'm proposing is difficult. I know that. So so difficult. But it is not *impossible*. Are we going to let the real opportunity of completing this endeavor in a satisfactory fashion slip away only because we are exhausted. Only because we are afraid.

How will we live with ourselves if we bring something into the world which isn't good enough.

We're not being paid enough to do shoddy work.

>*(There's a stunned, terrible silence.)*

>*(Into which, finally, **BEN** speaks.)*

BEN. *(Gently.)* Paul.

I don't think anything we do will ever be good enough.

Isn't that the condition, of the theater? I mean. Or if you're going to get general. Life.

It's too hard. It's too complex. It's too…much, of a task.

It's going to always lack.

There will always be a kind of failure

We have to find a beauty in that. To stay sane.

And I don't, honestly, I don't think Charles has the strength to know himself, and continue on. I don't… no. But. He still has to go through the other half of the play. So.

>*(There's a very long pause.)*

>*(Finally:)*

PAUL. Let's continue.

>*(He waves his hand.)*

Let's continue.

14.
ROCKET SCIENCE

(There's an elaborate transition taking place.)

STAGE MANAGER. I mentioned my degree in Rocket
    Science.

LIGHTS. You did.

> *(Lower.)*

Undergraduate.

STAGE MANAGER. What was that?

LIGHTS. It's an undergraduate degree, right?

STAGE MANAGER. Yes. In *Rocket Science.*

15.
CELLAR

CARSTAIRS. He says that you required him to whip you.

That you stripped to the waist, and that he whipped you.

(A beat.)

CHARLES. Yes, if it's of any interest.

CARSTAIRS. It is of interest, it's of more than interest, in certain currently very small circles it is a point of fascination.

CHARLES. I don't call you to account for all of your actions Carstairs. And thank god for you that I don't.

CARSTAIRS. For our friendship of course you don't.

CHARLES. I'll thank you not to go tampering about with mine.

CARSTAIRS. Do you understand anything Charles? Servants are not free standing lumps of clay they are human beings with human interests and they enjoy a gossip as much as the next person and servants, Charles, have masters.

CHARLES. All of this took place in the cellar. It was very private.

CARSTAIRS. In a cellar. Wonderful. There are, clubs, where a man may go with this sort of interest. They are very discrete.

CHARLES. This is not a sexual appetite! This is an inquiry.

CARSTAIRS. An inquiry into what, Charles. An inquiry into complete social humiliation? What ever made you think Peter could be trusted to keep his mouth shut. I've bribed him handsomely, you may pay me back thank you very much you would have botched the procedure. I've also threatened him and will continue to do so at irregular intervals. But you're going to have to raise his salary so that it's very high and you're going to have to keep it raised.

CHARLES. An inquiry into…an inquiry into… I hardly know how to say what.

CARSTAIRS. Charles, let me arrange an introduction for you.

CHARLES. For the last time, this is not…a depravity.

(**CHARLES** *hands him the letter; he reads it.*)

CARSTAIRS. Ah.

CHARLES. I should have liked to know what he experienced.

CARSTAIRS. Richard's adventure on the high seas. We can't any of us know. Oh don't look at me like that Charles, I don't trivialize it; Richard had an appetite for the transcendent that's why he took his whipping at high noon on a ship in the tropics surrounded by a circle of uneasy men, rather than in a basement in Chelsea. You can never know what he experienced. You haven't got his wild and bewildering heart.

CHARLES. But I can search for an approximation.

STAGE MANAGER. Standby, Lights 382

CARSTAIRS. You can playact, yes. But it is a piece of theater which will destroy you.

STAGE MANAGER. Lights 382 – go

(**LIGHTS** *start to dim.*)

(*But* **PAUL** *continues.*)

CARSTAIRS. And it won't be a romantic destruction like Richard's.

STAGE MANAGER. Hold.

CARSTAIRS. It will be the grimmest most trivial kind of social obliteration.

SOUND. Wait, did we get a rewrite?

STAGE MANAGER. *(Grim.)* No.

CARSTAIRS. Probably followed by a few torqued up passages in a diary and a suicide in a rented room. One of the commonest ways to die in a city.

But you are an extraordinary man, Charles, only in the eye of God. *(To the house:)* To whom we are all an astonishment. *(Back to* **CHARLES***.)* To the world, and in truth, you are a common person, inextricably bound up by mundane laws which I can assure you, you do not have the imagination or force of character to break.

How will you discover the kind of man you really are?

Climb for the highest place possible.

It will crumple beneath you, like a rotten bough, in spring. And your arms will swing, wildly, but they will not catch, and you will fall to the ground. And you will watch the petals tumble down towards broken you. Like snow. In your dying moments. In a great shower of light and white.

> *(There is a moment.)*

> *(***BEN*** reaches out to him.)*

BEN. Paul.

> *(***PAUL*** steps back, pulls his hand from his pocket, extends his hand, and runs his palm deliberately against the backdrop, leaving a smear of blood. He walks offstage.)*

16.
NEOSPORIN

STAGE MANAGER. *(To room.)* Going dark.

E2. *(From offstage.)* Thank you, dark!

DIRECTOR. Settle down everyone.

>   *(It all goes dark.)*

E2. If it's better to light a candle than curse the darkness, maybe it's easier to just *thank* the darkness.

SOUND. Okay I need quiet in the house. Total quiet in the house. I'm making a recording of the room tone.

E3. Do you know what's so wrong it just might be right? Olive bread, toasted. Pepper jelly *and* horseradish rare roast beef and manchego.

E2. *(Slightly hushed.)* Oh, I don't know, man.

E3. I think I might be on to something.

ASM. *(Slightly hushed.)* When I put that all together in my head it does not seem right.

E2. Agh

E3. Erik?

E2. Oh… I cut myself.

E3. *(Has adopted a lowered voice although it is unnecessary.)* You cut yourself

E2. With my trusty exacto.

E3. Do you need a bandaid? Because there's one in the kit.

E2. I don't…yeah. I don't know.

E3. Well put Neosporin on it or something at least I've seen your trusty exacto.

E2. It's actually. There's actually a lot of blood.

E3. Really? Already? How much?

E2. I think I cut it pretty deep…

E3. What were you *doing*?

ASM. Let me come see.

E2. Well it slipped. And…

E3. *(Joking.)* Stay with me. Stay with me Erik.

E2. Uh…

E3. Don't go into the light! There's a kit up here. You want an Aspirin or something also probably does it hurt

E2. Um… I mean yeah I guess it's more that it's throbbing

E3. Or an *ibuprofen.*

ASM. Alright, let me put some light on this situation… Okay that's a lot of blood. Let me get a paper towel I can't see…

E3. *(For the first time slightly concerned.)* How much blood/ *is* there?

E2. Aw man, I'm dripping it on the floor.

ASM. Okay. So. Let's – I'm going to put pressure on it for a moment. That's a lot of blood but I think…

E3. I think it's shallow cuts though, that bleed the most.

ASM. Okay…and now I'm going to take a look…okay wow. Yeah. This is…this is deep.

E2. It's pretty deep right?

ASM. It's deep.

E2. *(An utterance of flesh-revulsion and fear.)*

ASM. I actually think…you should go to the emergency room for this.

E3. You're kidding.

ASM. It's pretty deep. I think…yeah.

E2. Alright.

ASM. You should take a cab. You'll get reimbursed.

E3. How did you *do* that?

ASM. I'll let Molly know.

E2. No don't tell Molly!

SOUND. Backstage, I need total silence.

ASM. *(Even quieter.)* I've got to let Molly know.

E2. *(Even quieter.)* If you tell Molly she has to make me go.

ASM. Yeah but you do have to go.

E2. Yeah but I can't go right now.

ASM. You're bleeding pretty bad, Erik.

E2. You can't do the changeover for the split scene without me.

ASM. It'll be sort of ugly in the first preview but we'll work it Saturday and it'll be fine.

E2. Nothing can take twice as long right now.

ASM. Erik you have to go to the hospital.

E2. I am going to go to the hospital. I am totally going to go to the hospital. I'm just going to wait two hours, that's all.

E3. *(Also very quiet.)* Erik don't be ridiculous. Go to the hospital.

E2. It's just two hours. I'm not going to bleed out in a few hours. I'm using electrical tape. Look.

ASM. You're still bleeding.

E3. I'm going to let Molly know.

E2. *Don't.*

It's two hours. You can hold together a wound with electrical tape I totally saw that on some show about a man in the Gobi Desert. You can stop any wound with enough pressure. This is enough pressure. Don't tell Molly. Pretend I never told you. Okay I've got this. Electrical tape and paper towels. It's just two hours. Let's just get to the end of the night.

(Bit of a pause.)

E3. Neosporin. Make sure you put Neosporin in there.

17.
STORMY PETREL

CHARLES. They gave me his effects. A sketch of a stormy petrel. A notebook on which he'd written "Notes on Native Customs" and inside a few but only a very few notes on native customs. They said he'd once said that if anything ever happened to him, he'd want his best suit to go to the first mate, who happens to be his size.

And this is the last letter. Unfinished. Among the effects. He said: "This is the end of it all. A few clapboard houses and some natives. Meadows for two months in the summer; the rest of the year – ice. The edge of the world. The boundary of where man can live. I thought it would be some other thing, the farthest place, that it would be a spectacularity of a kind but it isn't, it's only less than what usually is."

(He closes his eyes.)

I feel unendurably close to you.

(He reaches out his hand. His fingers close around Nothing.)

Now that you're gone.

18.
END OF DAY/ PLAY

STAGE MANAGER. Ladies and gentlemen, we've come to the
last twenty-five minutes of the day please stay alert as
we are going to push through to the very last seconds
available to us. Please be sure to be here at 11 sharp
tomorrow morning bright-eyed and bushy-tailed and
ready to go as we're going to have a very long day's
work ahead.

> *(All the actors are on stage while something major
> is adjusted.)*

> *(There is a stream of technical information. Maybe
> all departments at once.)*

> *(**PAUL** stands alone, his expression is remote.)*

> *(**EVA** and **SIGET** are singing softly, a mellow folky
> melody:)*

EVA & SIGET.
UP AND OUT IN THE MORNING LIGHT
THE MOUNTAIN RISES ABOVE
UP AND OUT DO NOT CALL IT FLIGHT
I AM NOT RUNNING FROM
I AM RIDING TOWARDS
A GREATER LOVE

> *(**BEN** is talking with **JAKE** while **DIRECTOR**
> listens.)*

> *(**JAMIE** is on a ladder messing with a light. **E2** is
> holding the ladder and passing something up to
> her. His hand is almost mummified in olive green
> electrical tape.)*

> *(**PAUL** is onstage in full costume, sitting to the
> side.)*

> *(**PAUL** is thinking; we can hear it.)*

PAUL. When we were young. Before we belonged to unions. We would rehearse late into the night. We would drink after. And in the morning we would stumble into black pants, and leather shoes, and button up shirts, and ties sometimes, and go to our temp jobs where we would pretend we were envied because we were actors, but actually we were condescended to.

And when we got to tech, maybe the day before we opened, we would tech through the night, even though we could afford so few lights that we could only have so many cues, still, we were raw, and inexperienced, and didn't know what we were doing, and it would take all night, and there would be a fight, and one of the girls would storm into the bathroom in tears

One of the girls would storm into the bathroom in tears and all the other girls would gather around the bathroom and cope with it. One girl deputized to go in. Console. Rage with her against the director.

Someone might be drunk. Maybe someone was just a bit unhinged. Someone would start shouting. Someone would begin to sing. Everyone would sing.

When we stumbled out it was dawn. We were too tired to drink. The neighborhood might be still dangerous, at that hour, in the milky light. The last predators, the ones who were still hungry, detaching from a doorway and ambling forward with a slo motion nonchalance. We made our way home without being killed and we wanted more than anything to call it a night and to slip into bed, but we needed the complete paycheck too badly, or we had dropped too many days and were on probation with the temp agency, so we climbed into our black pants, our leather shoes, the shirt, which badly needed a wash, which needed to be ironed, we found the tie for some reason half underneath the radiator, scruffed with dust, and we put it all on, this sour smelling and crinkled ensemble, and we went to our clerical position, where only the copier girl noticed we looked like hell, and that night we went to the theater, and we opened the show.

And we knew that this was a splendid, a glorious way to live. We knew that this was the best way to live. Because we believed in what we were doing. Utterly. We believed in ourselves. Utterly. We were heroes of art. We were heroes.

> *(During* **PAUL***'s thought the other people on stage have slowly started to take up the song. Humming it, or singing along.)*

SONG.
> NEVER KNOW NEVER ASK
> AND NEVER SAY
> THE STREAM FLOWS FAST AND SILVERY
> THE MORNING STRETCHES OUT GLITTERY
> I AM RIDING TOWARDS CERTAIN VICTORY
> YES I KNOW IT IS CERTAIN VICTORY
> NEVER KNOW AND NEVER ASK AND NEVER SAY
> THERE IS NO HISTORY IN A NEW DAY
> I AM NO DEVIL NO I AM NOT A DEMON
> I AM NO DEVIL AND YOU ARE NOT A DEMON
> WE HAVE NOT DONE
> EACH OTHER ANY INJURY

> > *(The words and melody of the song mingle with the words and melody of the German Song and Goddesses and a lot of Technical Chatter.)*

> TWO-TWENTY-FOUR, RELEASE
> AND NEVER SEEN
> WITH SWINE NEVER SEEN WITH SWINE
> AND NOW THIRTY-TWO AT FIFTY-THREE
> AND WHY NOT TRY TWENTY-NINE AT SIXTY
> YES THAT'S GREAT TWENTY-NINE AT SIXTY
> NEVER SEEN NEVER SEEN NEVER SEEN WITH SWINE
> GODESSES GODESSES *DIE FI HEIN HEINST*
> *IST EIN HUNST* SCATTER ALL OF THE DARK AWAY
> AND NOW RELEASE
> RELEASE EVERYTHING

(And casual gestures have become a dance. Everyone on stage is dancing. The song might repeat.)

(Then everyone is singing all at once:)

I CANNOT KNOW WHAT I HAVE BECOME!
I ONLY KNOW IT IS SEALED AND DONE

I CANNOT KNOW WHAT I HAVE BECOME!
I CANNOT KNOW WHAT I HAVE BECOME!

(The dance continues. And the lights and sound and set do something very beautiful and initially strange but at the end complimentary.)

STAGE MANAGER. Ladies and Gentlemen, that's it for the night. You can all go home.

(Darkness.)